STREETWISE TAROT

Streetwise Tarot

Mark Lewis

Toronto

Mark Lewis Entertainment, Toronto, Canada
https://marklewisentertainment.com

© 2020 Mark Lewis
All rights reserved.

ISBN 978-0-9867329-1-1

Cover art, layout & design by Ariel Frailich

Contents

Foreword   *vii*

1. How I Became Psychic   1
2. The Major Arcana   19
    1. The Magician   24
    2. The High Priestess   25
    3. The Empress   25
    4. The Emperor   26
    5. The Hierophant   26
    6. The Lovers   27
    7. The Chariot   27
    8. Strength   28
    9. The Hermit   28
    10. Wheel of Fortune   29
    11. Justice   29
    12. The Hanged Man   30
    13. Death   30
    14. Temperance   31
    15. The Devil   31
    16. The Tower   32
    17. The Star   33
    18. The Moon   33
    19. The Sun   34
    20. Judgement   35
    21. The World   35
    22. The Fool   36
3. The Minor Arcana   37
    1. Wands   39
    2. Swords   41
    3. Cups   43
    4. Pentacles (Coins)   44
4. The Court Cards   51
    1. Queens   51
    2. Knights and Kings   52
    3. Pages   53

5. Ethics	55
6. Interpretation	69
The Pyramid Spread	74
The Celtic Cross	99
The Horoscope Spread	102
7. Money	107
Psychic Fairs And Kindred Events	108
Private Readings By Appointment	113
Psychic House Parties	116
Sound Recorded Internet Readings	117
Hotel Readings	118
8. A Party Trick	123

Foreword

Mark Lewis and I started corresponding sometime in the 1980s. He'd bought some books of mine as he was learning how to become a psychic reader. In what seemed like no time at all, he became the best-known psychic in Ireland. About thirty years ago, he moved to Toronto, Canada, where he's enjoyed a successful career as a palmist and Tarot card reader ever since.

We were friends well before we finally met at a marketing conference in Albuquerque in the early 1990s. We live in different parts of the world, but fortunately our paths have crossed a number of times over the years. Mark is a great raconteur with an excellent memory, and a wonderful sense of humour. Mark is also a gifted writer, as you'll soon discover. He has a breezy, easy-to-understand style, and his sense of humour is never far below the surface.

Mark works in a variety of settings, including flea markets, psychic fairs, and corporate events. He also has a thriving private practice. Consequently, his approach is different to that of other psychic readers, and he's happy to give you the benefit of his versatility and many years of experience. If you want to become a successful Tarot reader, you must read Mark's book.

> Richard Webster, *best-selling author of over 100 books on metaphysical subjects*
> Auckland, New Zealand
> October, 2020

CHAPTER ONE
How I Became Psychic

Despite the title of this opening chapter, I am not sure that the word "psychic" is really an appropriate one. Of course, it all depends on how you define the word "psychic" in the first place. I cannot read minds and I am not a carnival act when I do Tarot readings. If I could really know all, see all and tell all I could win the lotto! Come to think of it this also applies to every psychic I know who exhibits at psychic fairs! You should see them before the fairs start when they first arrive. They don't know where they are supposed to set up, which entrance they are supposed to enter and are always curious to find out who is on the next booth as their adjoining neighbor! All this reminds me of the old joke "Psychic fair cancelled because of unforeseen circumstances"!

In actual fact I believe the word "psychic" should really be defined as "heightened intuition". The problem is that I cannot go around calling myself a "heightened intuitionist" as it is a bit of a mouthful! I am therefore stuck with the word "psychic" for now. I suppose I could be a bit more sedate and call myself "a Tarot reader" and perhaps I should. After all, it does sound far more dignified!

I do believe everyone is psychic to some degree or other. If you accept my definition of the word as being nothing more than heightened intuition then it isn't such a mystery. Of course, it is also true that some people have stronger intuition than others. However, I also believe that intuition can be developed over a period of time and can often be triggered by certain occupations such as police and customs officers, sales people and obviously palm and Tarot readers.

With regard to the latter, the more readings you do, the more intuitive you become. Just dealing with people on an ongoing basis sharpens that intuition. The more you do it the more "psychic" you become.

I will probably, at some later point in this book, pontificate more on how and why I believe psychic ability really works. I don't believe there is anything mysterious about it. As I mentioned already, if you can accept my definition of the phenomenon as being merely heightened intuition, it can possibly make more sense and be more palatable to those of a skeptical disposition.

Tarot cards in particular are a marvelous tool for triggering off that intuition. I believe that it is the most powerful divination tool known to man. They are related to regular playing cards and I can never remember which came first, probably because I don't care that much! Besides, from my research, nobody really knows for sure anyway! Some authorities say that playing cards are derived from the Tarot and others claim it is the other way round! Since nobody really seems to know, I don't know why I am supposed to know either!

I do know that it is possible to read regular playing cards just as well as the Tarot. In fact, quite a few readers do it, in preference to the Tarot. The name for this is Cartomancy. In fact, although I have done a few Cartomancy readings myself, I far prefer the Tarot, since the images on the cards are more powerful and varied, especially the Major Arcana, which are the most important twenty-two cards of the Tarot.

While on the subject of playing cards, there is something uncanny about them. A deck of cards can almost be a calendar. Did you know that if you count the pips on a pack of cards, you will find three hundred and sixty-five? There are three hundred and sixty-five days in the year.

There are fifty-two cards in the deck, representing fifty-two weeks in the year. There are four suits, representing the four seasons. But things get really interesting when you count the deck to see if all fifty-two cards are there. Instead of counting in the usual way, as you deal each card spell one card for each letter thus:

A-C-E, T-W-O, T-H-R-E-E, and so on up to King. Spell the court cards, J-A-C-K, Q-U-E-E-N, K-I-N-G.

You will be amazed to see that the very last card spells out on the G of King. It works out exactly.

Here is the amazing part. Not only does this spelling enigma work in English, it also applies in French, Dutch, Swedish and German. For those of you who wish to amuse yourselves with this nonsense, please remember that "ch" counts as one letter in German.

Now we come to the real reason I have brought normal playing cards into the picture. They do have some relevance to this chapter in that, not only am I a palmist and Tarot reader, I am also a professional magician who specialises in card tricks!

In addition to performing on stage, I have also earned a portion of my income selling trick decks of cards at exhibitions, fairs and department stores in various countries. In my younger days, most of the venues I worked at were in Great Britain, where I lived at the time. The trick deck is called "the Svengali Deck" and I must have sold thousands and thousands of them. It is a spectacular demonstration and I would gather crowds around me, and at the end of the show, sell the product in question. I sold these decks in all sorts of odd places, including a waxworks!

However, there were other novelty venues that I decided to try. One was psychic fairs, where palmists, Tarot card readers, astrologers and other metaphysical people were plying their own unusual trade. I lived in Ireland at the time and these events were all located in England, so I travelled over to do them.

One psychic fair I worked was in Birmingham. Sales were good but there seemed to be a problem. My method of working was upsetting the neighboring psychics. They wanted to work quietly away and the slightest noise disturbed them. And of course, the noise they got from me wasn't the slightest. In addition, I also drew large crowds that they found distracting. I suppose it affected their psychic vibrations.

Suddenly, the promoter of the show confronted me and said, "You can't work like this. It affects the other exhibitors." I told her that there was no other possible way for me to work. I had to draw a crowd and I had to demonstrate. I promised to lower my voice if that would help but she would have none of it. She said, "Our other exhibitors don't draw people over in such an aggressive manner," and I responded, saying, "They are psychics. I am a demonstrator. Demonstrators use different sales techniques than psychics do."

She then retorted, "It won't do. You will have to move your table right back to the wall of your booth so that your crowd doesn't come into the aisle." I told her that if I moved my table back to the wall my sales would go down to zero but she insisted and I acquiesced. She moved my table right back to the wall and then disappeared.

Naturally, I moved it forward again once she had disappeared out of sight, but I forgot one thing. She was a psychic herself and must have gotten a vibe that I had pushed the table out again, so within a few moments, she reappeared and angrily said, "I told you to push your table back to the wall and you have pushed it back out again. We expect our exhibitors to cooperate with us, and if you are not going to do so, then we don't want you to come back next year."

She then stormed off in a great huff. I realized that the situation would have to be saved somehow so I ran after her and said, "I'll tell you what. To save any trouble next year I will come back and do what everyone else is doing. In other words, I will be a psychic. That way there will be no crowds and no loud demonstrations. I will work quietly away, just like everybody else."

She suspiciously responded, "Do you have any experience doing psychic readings?" I lied, saying that I had been doing it for twenty years, whereupon she enquired what kind of readings I did. I told her that I used Tarot cards and palmistry, which of course was a downright lie since I had never done a psychic reading in my entire life. She then said, "All right. You can come back next year and do psychic readings, but we don't want those trick cards back in here."

I figured that I would have a whole year, and that was plenty of time to figure out how to do readings. I had a vague notion that I would study the subject and fill in any gaps in my knowledge by simply making it all up, but in actual practice, I didn't do anything about it because of other commitments. However, as the exhibition approached, I started to wonder if I should go over to England and do it.

I was on the verge of chickening out when I got a phone call from the promoter wanting to know if I was going to exhibit this year. Since I was caught on the hop I impulsively said yes. However, I didn't actually send any money for the booth rental as they requested. I still wasn't sure that I should exhibit since I really had made no preparation or study to do psychic readings. I deliberately didn't send any money or sign the contract because of this.

However, nearer the date I got another phone call demanding money and the signed contract back. I stalled, saying that the show was starting very soon and, by the time I mailed a cheque from Ireland and by the time she cashed it, I would be in Birmingham anyway. I told her that I would pay her in cash on the opening day of the fair. She reluctantly went along with this. I then felt obliged to attend, notwithstanding the fact that the fair was only a few days away and I had made no preparation or had any experience in the art of psychic readings.

I decided that the best way to handle things was to learn a script that would fit anyone and everyone. I noticed from my acquaintance with Blackpool seaside fortune tellers that this is precisely what they did. Of course, the gypsy fortune tellers in Blackpool were a far cry from the more serious readers in Birmingham, but I reasoned that it would probably work.

I therefore wrote out a script that I would say to everyone regardless of who they were. The only trouble was that I found that learning the script off by heart in the limited time span I had was damn near impossible, so I soon gave up that idea. Instead, I had a half-baked idea in my mind that I would secrete the written script in my lap as I did the reading. My idea was that I would read the script in my lap and the client wouldn't know the difference.

I then made up a few signs proclaiming that I was a psychic and purchased a plane flight to Birmingham. However, on the flight I had quite severe misgivings about the whole concept and I changed my mind in mid-flight. I figured that I would never get away with it and talked myself out of the whole idea. I decided instead that once I got to Birmingham, I would have a few days off and make a holiday of it. My brother lived in Birmingham and I would take the opportunity to visit him instead of attending the psychic fair. After all, I hadn't signed a contract or paid any money, so I could get out of the agreement to exhibit very easily. When I made my decision, I relaxed completely and the weight of becoming a psychic when I actually wasn't one was taken off my shoulders.

I checked into my Birmingham hotel and I discovered that it was quite near the hall where the psychic fair was being held. I resolved that I would visit the fair but not exhibit. I just wanted to have a look but now had no intention of setting up there. I figured that I would make myself scarce if I happened to see the promoter there. My plan was to disappear before she saw me.

However, as Robert Burns, the great Scottish poet once stated, "The best laid plans of mice and men gang aft agley". For those of my readers that do not speak the Scottish language, it simply means that plans sometimes go wrong, as they did in this case, since, on wandering round the hall and congratulating myself on deciding not to exhibit, I felt a tap on my shoulder, and when I looked round, I saw the psychic fair promoter glaring at me. She said, "I need some money from you before you set up." Alas and alack, I was now caught red-handed and I didn't have the nerve to tell her that I had changed my mind about exhibiting, since she would have been furious and, being a psychic herself, would probably have put a hex on me. I duly paid up and resigned myself to two days of being a rookie psychic.

I put up my display signs that I had brought with me and sat at the table that had been provided. I remember charging five pounds for the reading, which would have been about fifteen minutes or so in duration. This would have been about thirty-five years or so ago. Nowadays, at the time of writing this (2020), at a psychic fair I would charge eighty Canadian dollars (around fifty pounds) for about twenty minutes to half an hour, which shows that times and prices have moved on.

Of course, I had then to decide how to do a reading when I had no psychic power whatsoever. I still had the little script with me, and I decided that this, combined with a bit of astute guesswork, would be enough to do a successful psychic reading.

I sat there in abject fear, hoping and praying that nobody would sit down and have a reading, and started to curse my stupidity for attempting this nonsense. I felt that all the psychics were looking at me and thinking, "That was the fellow who was doing card tricks last year. How come he has suddenly become psychic?"

And then I got my first paid customer for a psychic reading and I remember her to this day. She was in her mid-twenties and even more stressed out than I was. She was literally shaking with nerves. I could see that she was trembling and on the edge of tears. I used a deck of regular playing cards for the reading but had no idea of the divinatory meaning of the individual cards. I asked her to select ten and I laid them out in a spread.

I didn't actually have to look at the script on my lap and since I could see that she was very stressed out the reading was very easy for me. Her body language and my streetwise cunning showed me what was on her mind. I was able to waffle successfully for about fifteen minutes and she seemed pleased with the reading, and more importantly, the message I imparted, which was designed to give her courage and hope.

After she departed I left my stand to go outside in the fresh air to relieve my tension and meditate upon what I had just done. It was my first paid reading ever and I remember being a bit upset over it, even though it had been quite successful. I had no idea that people would be in such distress in their lives and it bothered me. To this day, I still get upset over other people's stresses and strains.

I remember a psychic once telling me that "the best psychics are the ones who have had hard lives." There might be something in the statement, since someone who has had it hard has empathy with fellow sufferers and, as I was soon to learn, clients don't go to a psychic when things in their lives are hunky-dory. They visit when things in their lives are not quite right. Of course, there are the short entertainment readings that sometimes people will do at a party on a non-professional basis, but once a reading lasts more than ten minutes and money changes hands, then the odds are that the client is in trouble of some sort.

This first reading distressed me because of the troubles that this young lady had. I resolved that as soon as this fair was over, I would never get involved in this work again. Alas, something went wrong with my resolution, because since that day, I have done thousands upon thousands of readings over a period of thirty-five years or so. And many of these readings have been far more distressing than this first one I did in Birmingham so many years ago.

After walking around the block for half an hour to relieve my stress, I felt strong enough to go back into the fair and continue my charade. Eventually another client sat down and I did another reading which was not quite as successful as the first. There was no trembling this time and no body language to give me an idea of what was going on in this person's life. I tried to read the script in my lap but I couldn't bloody see it properly, so that idea was a washout. However, I came out with some waffle for around fifteen minutes and the client did not look too pleased when she paid me.

Again I went outside to relieve my tension after this reading. I remember thinking, "How the hell did I get into this?" Come to think of it, I am still considering that question to the present day.

Over the course of the day I did about seven readings, most of which weren't bad, but one or two were distinctly iffy and the clients did not look very pleased. I was also having great trouble with the written script. Since I discovered that I couldn't read it in my lap, I decided to stick it to the inside of the table with some wax. I felt very vulnerable doing this because the paper became much more visible. I also kept imagining that the neighboring psychics would see it and would be very disapproving of my wicked ways.

The question soon became moot, since the damn paper kept coming off and falling to the floor. I therefore had to do without the script and make the whole reading up as I went along. My experience as a magic demonstrator helped me quite a bit with this, as did my knowledge of people coupled with my street smarts, having lived among rogues and vagabonds at various points in my life. However, that is another story for another time!

I went back to the hotel that evening with the little piece of paper that kept falling to the floor and tried to put some work into memorizing it properly in preparation for the next day, which would be the final one, since it was a two-day fair. I also said a little prayer for the first girl that I had read. I just couldn't get her out of my mind and I felt that I had to pray for her. I am a very odd person because I don't believe in God but I pray anyway. God knows why. And you can read that last sentence in any way you want.

I ventured forth the next day, relieved that it would all soon be over. I used to dread customers, so I wouldn't encourage them. I used to look away and avoid eye contact and hoped that they wouldn't sit down with me, and for the most part, they didn't. If I had truly wanted customers, I would have done very well financially and would have had many more readings. However, I was in such abject terror of the whole procedure that business was slow for me. I would waste a lot of time going outside after every reading to calm down and, of course, this affected business, too.

Still, despite my best efforts to deter customers, I actually got a few, whether I wanted them or not. Most of the readings weren't bad at all, since I had memorized the script a bit better. An odd one or two were awful, but I was encouraged because a few people complained to me about the other psychics, too. The fact that the other psychics were getting moans and groans about their bad readings made me feel that I wasn't alone.

After a few hours I decided to go on my usual trip outdoors, but just when I reached the exit door, an exuberant girl in her twenties covered in jewelry asked me, "Are you Mark Lewis?" I was quite astonished by this, since my name was displayed nowhere on my stand and I had no literature there with my name on it either. I answered her in the affirmative and she enquired, "Are you going out? I wanted a reading."

I felt instinctively that this would be an easy reading so I replied, "I don't have to go out. I can do a reading now if you want me to."

She was delighted to hear this, so we headed back to my stand and on the way, I asked her how she knew my name. She responded, gushing, "Oh, my friend had a reading with you yesterday and she said that you were absolutely marvelous and you were a great help to her. She has been going through a really bad time lately and she said that you made her feel much better. She asked you your name yesterday and she gave it to me to come and see you. She thoroughly recommended you."

I then put two and two together and realized that her friend was the first person who came to me the day before; the one that was a nervous wreck and that I had felt the urge to pray for the night before.

Armed with that knowledge and the fact that this girl in front of me was so accepting and easy to read made this one of my most successful readings of the fair. She paid me and at the same time praised me to the skies and kept chattering about how wonderful I was.

She departed and I again started to make my usual escape to the fresh air outside. However, when I got to the exit, she was there again, but this time with an older woman. She said to me, "You're not going out again, are you? I want you to do a reading for my mother." The older woman was indeed her mother, but I am afraid that she didn't look the slightest bit enthusiastic about having a reading, and in fact, she looked so miserable that I hoped she wouldn't.

Actually, she did refuse and said haughtily, "I don't need a reading." However, her daughter pleaded and begged with her, saying, "Mother, he is absolutely marvelous. I have never come across anyone as good as him!"

Unfortunately, this made the mother look quite resentful and it was plain that she had no interest whatever in having a reading. I didn't want to read her and she didn't want to be read by me, so you would think this would result in a happy mutual arrangement not to bother each other.

However, the daughter insisted and cajoled so much that the woman reluctantly consented. I went back to my table accompanied by her with a feeling of great foreboding. As I sat down, I had a bad feeling altogether and she confirmed it by exuding negativity galore, which quite unsettled me. Her entire body language indicated that she did not want to be there and considered me to be an inferior psychic. On this occasion she was right because my reading was way off base and I got it all wrong.

In the end I made such a mess of things that I said to her, "I am sorry. I can't get any vibes through. I just can't read you. Let me return your money." She softened and said, "That is all right, dear. That sort of thing happens when you do a reading. It happens to me from time to time, too." I got a little confused by this and responded, "It happens to you? Do you do readings yourself?" She smirked and told me her name in such a manner that she expected me to know it. She then went on, "I am a professional clairvoyant, dear."

I then asked her if she had a booth at the fair and she looked quite insulted, saying, "I don't do readings at fairs, dear. My clients are exclusive and I do readings internationally." I responded, "Oh, no wonder I couldn't read you. I can't seem to do it with other psychics."

She responded, "Don't worry, dear. I can. I know all about you, for example." She then started to show off her great superiority by rattling off a whole bunch of facts about me, which shocked me with their accuracy. Then she said, "You are going down to the seaside in a few days, aren't you?" To this day I have no idea how she knew that because, in fact, I intended to visit Great Yarmouth in Norfolk to visit a friend of mine who lived and worked there. It is indeed a seaside resort on the east coast of England.

She went on, "One day you will live in Canada and have a son there." She got that half right, since I am, at the time of writing, indeed living in Canada. I don't have a son, though, and I don't think it is likely to happen. However, she did pretty well and I was greatly impressed. I tried to figure out how she knew those things. At first, I wondered for a moment if I had said something to her daughter about my life, but I knew perfectly well that I didn't. I then went over the memory of her daughter's friend who came in the day before and I was quite certain that I had said nothing there either that would give away information. I later realized that I had met a genuine psychic who had no need of hidden scraps of paper or reliance on body language and a gift of the gab.

I finished up the fair later that day, still in a great state of awe and wonder. However, the amazing sequel came a couple of years later when I was in a bookshop browsing through a volume in the New Age section. This book consisted of mini-biographies of famous psychics. Lo and behold, there was a photograph of her staring right at me! And there were also a few pages written about her. Unfortunately, this happened so many years ago that I have quite forgotten the woman's name or the name of the book she was in. It was quite a surprise, though.

When I returned to Dublin, I resolved that I would never indulge in psychic readings again. I had made no profit from the fair but I hadn't lost money either. The whole exercise was just a break-even proposition, although it certainly had been a fascinating experience. In any event I didn't feel comfortable with this weird way of making a living.

I lived in Blackpool, England, at one time. It was and still is a big resort seaside town in Britain. I did know from my days there that psychic readings were a profitable business. I knew a few of the gypsy seaside fortune tellers and was familiar with the way they operated and the money they made.

There was also an incident that I remember when I was walking along a Blackpool beach with a streetwise hustler called Bruce. He kept picking up pebbles and I asked him what he was doing. He said that he was picking up the pebbles for his "clients". I had no idea what he was talking about and asked him to explain. It seemed that he did mail-order readings on a cassette tape recorder and sent the tapes to the client along with a lucky charm. The charm in question was one of these pebbles on the beach! He called it a lucky stone and told the clients it would be a blessing for them and would bring them good fortune. They certainly brought Bruce good fortune at any rate!

I forgot all about the psychic business for a couple of years, but one day I decided to try the mail order idea of Bruce's without the lucky pebble aspect. I reasoned that the advantage of only doing it by mail was that I would not have to go through the terror of actually being in the client's presence and could turn off the tape recorder if I got stuck without something to say. I could then resume when I gathered my thoughts and thought of some further waffle.

This time, however, I resolved to study the matter properly and started to learn palmistry from books. To my amazement, when I tried it out on friends, it turned out to be remarkably accurate and I realized that it was quite a genuine method of divination that went back thousands of years. In fact, palmistry is actually mentioned in the Bible. In any event, I decided that if I were going to do readings, I would be on a surer footing if I were to do things the genuine way and rely less on guesswork in the way I did at Birmingham.

When I decided that I was competent enough to do the readings for money, I advertised in various magazines that I could do palmistry by mail order. Now my reader is wondering how it is possible to do palmistry by mail. No, the clients didn't have to cut their hands off and send them to me by post! Instead I would get them to send me a photocopy of their palms and I would send them back a taped reading based on what I saw on the photocopy. I would tell the client not to press too hard on the glass when making the photocopy and when they did that, quite a good copy of their hand emerged.

To go off on a little tangent here, it is quite interesting that if you take a copy of your palm print as indicated above and then take a similar copy a year later, you will see that there have been some subtle changes in the lines. Some will have disappeared and some new ones will have appeared. Sometimes the lines will develop breaks in them or they may become either stronger or weaker. The lines on the palm are always moving and growing as the person's life changes.

I made a little money from these mail order readings but certainly not a fortune. I did get feedback that the readings were terribly accurate. It was beginning to dawn upon me that palmistry was a very real method of divination.

During this period I decided to bring over to Ireland a young Canadian magician named Adam Harmes. Nowadays, Adam is a distinguished professor who is going to be somewhat less distinguished now that I have decided to include him in this book. Adam used to work in Canada for me and I would tell him stories about Ireland. Finally, I thought it would be a good idea to bring him over from Canada to help me with my work.

He worked the summer of 1987 with me in Ireland. Alas, we didn't do that well with the Svengali deck mainly because of the lack of suitable venues in Ireland, so we were both running low on money. I tried to figure out how to make some money quickly and I hit on the idea of becoming psychic again.

I had an untidy office in Dublin that Adam always used to refer to sarcastically as "corporation headquarters". The office was costing me rent so I thought I might as well make use of it. I thought that it might be a good idea to do readings in the office. I told Adam that my plan was to place a classified advertisement in the newspaper saying, "Famous psychic arriving in Dublin. Half hour taped readings. Phone for appointment at...." And then I filled in the phone number.

Adam, in his usual cynical manner, scoffed that I wouldn't get a single call. I told him that it would be worth a try. And it certainly was. We were both taken by surprise at the response. To my utter astonishment, about a hundred people called for appointments within the first week of running the advertisement. Many of them didn't show up for the session, but a hell of a lot did. Before I knew where I was, I was rushed off my feet with readings.

The only snag was that some of my sessions weren't very good and I got very mixed receptions as to my psychic ability. Some people thought that I was wonderful but a great many thought that I wasn't. I made sure to get paid in advance because of this. Despite the negative reactions of many to the readings, I was very busy indeed and was becoming financially solvent once again.

The main problem with the readings was that I was quite inexperienced and was trying to bluff my way through it. After a year and a half, the readings had improved to a great extent, especially when I studied how to read Tarot cards, but in the beginning, some of the results were abysmal. I knew I had potential talent in this area, since many of the clients were very happy, but I would say that fully one-third weren't. However, because of my streetwise experience I managed to get by without blinking too much of an eyelid at the dissatisfied customers. Of course, a thick skin developed from years of selling Svengali decks helped considerably.

On one memorable day, however, things came to a head with the bad readings. I had three appointments booked in one after the other. The first was a lady who was alone and the other two were a mother and daughter who had come together.

The first reading went badly and I could see that the woman wasn't satisfied. I resolved to get rid of her as quickly as possible and away she went with her money safely in my pocket. Then the two other women appeared, mother and daughter, and I took the daughter first. She was underwhelmed by the reading and it showed in her body language and general attitude. However, as always, I had her money and wasn't too concerned. I then dismissed her and brought her mother in while she waited outside.

Unfortunately, unbeknown to me, trouble was brewing. The first lady had left the premises, no doubt fretting about how bad a reading she had, and how the awful psychic had scammed her. She decided to return and ask for her money back. She met Adam in the waiting area, who told her that she would have to see me about that.

However, in the waiting area was sitting the daughter of the woman who was in having a reading. She had just had a reading herself from me and was also dissatisfied. When she heard the other lady complain they compared notes and decided that I was a complete fraud and they both conspired together to make an almighty fuss and get their money back when I came out. They both harassed Adam to give them a refund, but he refused to take the responsibility for it.

Of course, nowadays he pontificates about economics as a university professor. I am glad to see that he got his first education in these matters from working with me. He realized that it would not be an advantage to him personally if he gave these women a refund. Very astute of him, if I may say so, and good training for his future career as a professor who later wrote books about money-related matters.

However, Adam also realized that it might not be a good thing for me to come out and face two irate women without some warning. He therefore went outside to a pay phone to call and warn me of impending trouble. Unfortunately, when the phone rang in my office, I ignored it as a courtesy to the lady I was reading at the time.

Adam was nothing if not persistent and resourceful, so he climbed up on to a neighboring roof and repeatedly threw stones and pebbles at my window to get my attention. I excused myself to the client and went to the window to see what on earth was going on. I looked out and saw Adam on the roof next door, frantically trying to signal to me by sign language that something was amiss. I had no idea what he was trying to convey since I wasn't really psychic, so I merely ignored him by shrugging my shoulders and went back to work.

The lady I was reading was mightily impressed and was far more receptive than her daughter, and I thought that all was well. When I opened the door, however, I was to find two irate women snapping at me and demanding their money back. They were threatening all sorts of dreadful scenarios if I didn't refund the money, such as contacting the consumer protection authorities and the press.

I decided that the least troublesome option was to just give the money back and get rid of them. However, the mother who had the good reading looked terribly uncomfortable and told her daughter not to make such a fuss and that she was quite happy with her reading. The poor woman then scampered outside in great embarrassment, leaving me with the two battle axes.

I handed them their money back and just waited for them to go, but the daughter said, "Now, what about the money for my mother's reading? I want that back as well." I refused, saying, "Your mother was quite happy with her reading. If she comes back to me herself and wants a refund, she can have it. However, I can't let you speak for her." Of course, I knew that the mother wouldn't be back to me.

Eventually I got rid of them and I resolved that, from now on, there would be no more complaints, and from that day forth I studied divination methods properly. In fact, I spent hours and hours studying astrology, palmistry, Tarot, auras, numerology, rune stones and every divination system you can think of. At one point, my psychic book collection became bigger than my conjuring library.

In addition to this, I studied books on counseling and tried to develop my own true psychic ability. I believe everyone has this ability, but when you do it all the time as a professional clairvoyant, your intuition and innate psychic ability sharpen. As the old saying goes, "Practice makes perfect."

As time went by, I seemed to know all about people just by looking at them. I just knew what was going on in their lives. I would get flashes of names and situations that I couldn't possibly know about and they turned out to be correct. All my shenanigans and trickery went out the window and it was no longer necessary to use them. In fact, I was far better off without them, and the moment I abandoned that nonsense was the moment my intuition started to sharpen.

It is a very odd thing in the psychic business that skeptics become believers when they start to do readings themselves. And the longer they do readings, the more they believe in it. Many people come into the business just wanting to make money, but not really believing in it.

Before very long, however, they find that there *is* something in it and they end up with a lot of faith in metaphysical matters. That is precisely what happened to me.

One surprising offshoot of all this spirituality is that it made me a more understanding and compassionate person and transformed the hardened, unscrupulous hustler in me to a softer, kinder human being.

In the early days, however, some of my readings were a bit hit or miss. Among the more memorable and thankfully successful ones, I can remember a few examples.

There was one lady whose dog had been killed by a person unknown and my client wished me to contact the said canine in the spirit world and ask it the identity of the perpetrator of this dreaded deed. I did indeed contact the dog, who had somehow acquired the ability to speak English in the spirit world and who gave a good description of the person who was guilty of the atrocity. Unfortunately, the dog wasn't able to provide the name, address and phone number of the assailant. The psychic world of the animal kingdom does have its limitations, I suppose.

Then there was the lady who believed that she was herself psychic. There had recently been the murder of a child reported prominently in the Irish newspapers of the time and this lady was convinced that the mother was the perpetrator. In fact, she had gone down to the police station and insisted to the detective in charge of the case that she had psychic abilities and insisted that he arrest the mother of the child. The officer in question had some doubts as to the lady's psychic ability or indeed her sanity and declined to cooperate.

The woman then came to me and wanted my opinion of the matter. I told her that she might be right but then she might also be wrong, which of course covered both eventualities and was 100% accurate. She seemed happy with that and made me promise that once I got a more certain vision of the guilty person that I contact the detective in charge of the case. She dutifully wrote down the phone number of the police officer, handed it to me and departed my office, leaving her money behind in my pocket, which of course was of more concern to me than solving a crime that was more properly left to the authorities to figure out.

Another memorable reading was of a young man who seemed happy with the session, but yet I felt that there was something troubling him that hadn't yet come out in the reading. I asked him if I had covered everything he wanted to know and he said "yes". However, I still got the feeling that he wasn't telling me everything.

Anyway, at the end of the reading I accompanied him downstairs because I knew the door to the premises was locked on this one occasion, and I would have to let him out. We made small talk and just as we got to the door he said, "Oh, can I ask you just one more question?" I knew that now what was really bothering him would be revealed, so I replied, "Yes, of course."

He then floored me by saying, "Can people read my mind?" I said, "What makes you say that?" and he responded by saying, "There are a few people I know and I think they can read my mind and I don't like it." I then assured him that nobody could read his mind, including even me or any other psychic, for that matter. He asked if I was sure of this and I assured him that I was 100% certain. He looked greatly relieved at this and I knew immediately he had gotten value for money from the reading. Incidentally, I believe that I was correct in my assessment of the situation. I really do believe that people could not read his mind.....

Adam went back to Canada and I continued to improve my readings and genuine psychic ability. I studied and studied and studied. I discovered the Tarot during this period and found it so powerful that my business skyrocketed. I eventually expanded my readings from a half-hour session to an hour and charged more money for it. I became very good at what I did and achieved massive publicity in Ireland as a psychic, with many newspaper articles, and I appeared on many television and radio programs as a psychic consultant.

I read for noted entertainers, politicians and people of celebrity status. I was swamped with requests for readings and I became very well known indeed from massive newspaper articles that were written about my work. Some of the articles were a full page long and there were even a few two-page spreads.

In 1988, the late but famous pop star Michael Jackson came to Ireland to tour and the newspapers asked me to do an astrology reading for him from his date of birth. I did not meet him personally. I put this on a cassette audio tape and gave one copy to the paper. It got me a full page write-up in the newspaper, and from that point on, I was booming with business. I tried to get the audiotape to Michael Jackson through various intermediaries. I am not sure if he ever received it.

I interspersed my readings with children's magic shows and the advantage of this was twofold. One, the ordeal of dealing with the sadness of people's lives contrasted well with the fun of entertaining children, and two, it was a very easy matter to schedule the readings in-between the shows. The shows were fixed dates, but the readings could be arranged to my convenience.

I ended up writing horoscopes for newspapers, which I found very tedious indeed. I did this in conjunction with various psychic phone lines that I had arranged. These were voice-activated by the client and very general readings, but they did raise my psychic profile and brought in decent revenue that at least I didn't have to work for.

However, my most powerful divination tool was easily the Tarot. I studied it thoroughly and, in fact, I am still studying it, since there is no limit to its mysteries. All the trickery and wickedness of thirty-five years ago that I have described in this chapter is no more. It just isn't necessary anymore.

Nevertheless, I believe the street smarts involved has strangely made my readings more powerful. If you know how life works, you get to know how people's minds work. I do believe that once you get to know how people's minds work, you then get to have an understanding of how the Tarot works. Call it life experience if you like.

The purpose of this opening chapter, apart from entertaining the reader and getting this book off to a good start, is to give you an idea why I have called this book *Streetwise Tarot*. I believe you can be streetwise but intuitive at the same time. In fact, I believe that one helps the other. I will try to impart some of that in the pages to come.

CHAPTER TWO
The Major Arcana

Let's get down to business. I suppose I had better try to explain how I believe the Tarot actually works. Or should I say, the streetwise way that it works. There are myriad non-streetwise ways, of course, but I like to be a bit different. Now, I am not saying that the non-streetwise methods are invalid. There are some excellent Tarot readers who follow these methods and do pretty well with them. There are really no rights or wrongs in this business, providing you give good readings that help people rather than harm them.

So how does the Tarot work? Or to put it more accurately, how do I personally think it works? I am too cynical a person to believe that it works because of some unseen spirits hovering over the cards or that there is some centuries-old mystical reason behind it that is now lost in history. Some readers believe it works on Jung's theory of synchronicity but I certainly don't—even if I knew what the hell the theory actually is!

I believe the Tarot works on perfectly logical principles that even a skeptic might accept. It's a little difficult to explain but I shall gird up my loins and attempt to do so. Each card in a Tarot deck represents something that is relevant to everyone's life. I repeat the word "everyone" as it is very relevant to the point I am trying to make.

Let me take one card as an example; let's say the Chariot card. Now, this card means (to me anyway), "victory after a struggle". Of course, this specific card might mean something else to a different Tarot reader but we will come to that later. For now, let us stick to my own meaning.

Think about it. *Everyone* you do a reading for will have had at some time (or is going to have) "victory after a struggle"!

Or let us take the Two of Swords. To me that means conflict (swords crossing). Well, who doesn't have conflict in their lives sooner or later? Let me try one more. In fact, right now I have a deck right in front of me spread on the table face down. I will select one card at random. One moment please. Ah! The Ten of Wands. To me that means the end of confusion. Well, think about it. Everyone gets confused at times, and sooner or later, the confusion ends. Or at least I hope so!

So, do you get the idea? Every card in the pack applies to everyone in some way. Now, when you lay out a spread, no matter who the Querent is, the cards will apply to that person. It doesn't matter who they are. I have often said that a spread of cards randomly selected could fit Mother Teresa just as well as Adolf Hitler!

Lest you lift a quizzical eyebrow at this bold statement, I shall illustrate it with just one card. Let us say the Chariot Card, as already discussed, for example. As I already mentioned, it means (to me anyway), "victory after a struggle". However, to Mother Teresa, it could mean victory over poverty. To Adolf Hitler, it could mean victory in the war. (Yes, yes, I know it didn't happen, but let's not get too technical!)

The point I am trying to make is that, no matter what card shows up, it can relate to a client's life in some way. And of course, it also follows from this that a spread of say, ten cards, will do exactly the same thing! A little more complex than just one card certainly, but the principle remains the same.

However, to complete the job, you can't just go by the meaning of the card or cards. You have to add in the interpretation of the spread in front of you and relate it somehow to the person that you are reading. That is where the real art of reading the Tarot comes in—the *interpretation!*

In any event, I will delve into that in more detail later on in this book. For the moment, I am just trying to explain how I believe the Tarot works. No mystical or esoteric, weird spiritual reasoning. Just common sense and perfectly logical. I do concede that this may be a disappointment to some of my more metaphysically-minded readers, but that, after all, is the reason that this book has been given the title *Streetwise Tarot!*

To attempt further to sum up what I am trying to convey is that the Tarot acts as a random stimulator. The cards come up at random and are not pre-ordained by some mystical force to come up in a spread, as some Tarot practitioners believe. They act as a stimulator to your own mind and trigger off both your imagination and your intuition. However, this won't work unless you have someone in front of you to stimulate that imagination and intuition. You have to fit that stimulation to the person you are doing the reading for.

For example, if you have a dour, serious person in front of you and the Sun card shows up, you cannot say to him or her that, "You have a sunny disposition," in the same way that you can if you have a happy, effervescent person sitting down with you! Instead, you would have to say something like, "Life has not always been easy for you, but the Sun card shows that there is going to be improvement ahead." Something like that anyway!

Incidentally, the Sun card does not necessarily have to mean a sunny disposition. In fact, I don't really use that definition myself, although I certainly could if I wanted. I was merely trying to give an example of how you should try to fit the meanings of the cards to the person you are reading for.

In actual fact, the Sun card is generally a very positive card to most Tarot readers, and to me, it is the best card in the deck. It means success, victory and good things happening. However, we will get to that a bit later. Right now, I just want you to digest my theory as to why the Tarot works. It is really an exercise in creative thinking rather than some mystical esoteric power—to me anyway! There are many other philosophies around that will be diametrically opposite to that which I have espoused above, but since I am the one writing this book you will have to put up with my viewpoint for the moment!

Now, I mentioned earlier that every Tarot reader seems to have different meanings for each card. Many of them use the traditional meanings that have lived through the centuries but put their own spin on the matter. It is a fact that if you read through many books on the Tarot, you will see a lot of contradictory meanings, as well as some that do actually agree with each other. This can quite confuse rookie students of the Tarot. They may well say, "Well, which meaning am I supposed to use?"

I have no idea what answer other authors would give but I certainly know what my response is. Hold on to your hats, folks! This might horrify traditional Tarot theorists, but I stick by it nevertheless. Use any meaning you like! The first thing I advise people to do is to tear up the little white book that comes with the deck and form your own meanings! The Tarot will still work and, in fact, probably work better, since you are using meanings that mean something to *you*.

I suppose I shouldn't really advise you to tear up the little white book, as it may well be thought of as an example of wanton cruelty to a little book of instructions that has never done anybody any harm. OK, I will accept that, so go ahead and read it but don't take the meanings explained in the booklet too seriously. Use it as a guide and see if there are any meanings that resonate with you. And do the same with other Tarot books. Read them and digest what the authors give as their meanings as a bit of a guideline rather than anything cast in tablets of stone.

Then, the next thing you do is to find a quiet spot where you will not be disturbed, take each card one at a time, meditate on it and form your own meaning for that particular card. Decide what it means to YOU! Repeat this for every other card in the deck.

Of course, one of the biggest obstacles to learning the Tarot is trying to memorize the meanings of all seventy-eight cards. It is easier than you think if you use mnemonics. Now I suppose I had better explain what "mnemonics" are! Essentially, it means memory tricks that can help you remember things more easily. I will explain all that a little later. For now, let us just concentrate on the twenty-two cards of the Major Arcana.

At this point, I should explain that a Tarot deck consists of twenty-two cards of what is known as the Major Arcana and fifty-six cards known as the Minor Arcana—seventy-eight cards altogether. The Minor Arcana is made up of four suits consisting of fourteen cards per suit. The suits are Wands, Cups, Coins and Swords. The Major Arcana has no suits at all.

Traditionally, the Minor Arcana is supposed to mean small incidents and changes in a person's life, whereas the Major Arcana is supposed to mean larger and more meaningful influences. Or at least that is one theory anyway. Alas, I have found that, in studying the Tarot, you get all sorts of theories often contradicting each other, depending on who came up with the theory, and it is pretty difficult to figure out which is which. I shall therefore advise you to cut through the maze and simply read what I have to say on the matter instead! After all, I know all, see all and will tell all!

The simplest definition is that the Major Arcana is far more powerful than the Minor Arcana, and let us leave it at that! In fact, there are some readers who abandon the Minor Arcana altogether and just work with the Major Arcana!

Anyway, let's not worry about the Minor Arcana right now! I will cover it in more detail in the next chapter. After all, the Minor Arcana is a bit more complicated to explain, since not only are there more cards to worry about, but the designs and the meanings vary from deck to deck, depending on the brand of Tarot deck used. Luckily, the Major Arcana has pretty much the same design, no matter which type of Tarot deck is used.

For the moment, I will assume the Rider-Waite deck is the one that the student of this book is going to use, as it is the most popular and generally available Tarot deck out there. I believe that it is probably the best one for a beginner to make use of, as the images on the cards are very vivid, which in itself makes them easier to remember.

The Major Arcana cards are as follows:

1. The Magician
2. The High Priestess
3. The Empress
4. The Emperor
5. The Hierophant
6. The Lovers
7. The Chariot
8. Strength
9. The Hermit
10. Wheel of Fortune
11. Justice
12. The Hanged Man
13. Death
14. Temperance
15. The Devil
16. The Tower
17. The Star
18. The Moon
19. The Sun
20. Judgement
21. The World
22. The Fool

Now, as I have already stated, I believe that it is up to you to decide which meaning you should ascribe to each card. To help you along, I will give you my own meanings with a little variation or two. Of course, as I already explained, you can use any meaning you like that particularly resonates with you. Look at the pictures on the cards and see if anything stirs your imagination and creativity. In other words, you don't have to use my suggestions, but pick out something that is more meaningful to you. However, the reason I am going to explain my own meanings for the cards is twofold; first, because it can be a good starting point for you, and secondly, I can give you some memory tricks so that you can remember the meanings more quickly!

So here is the list again, what meaning I personally ascribe to each card and how to remember that meaning.

1. The Magician

I generally see this as a professional person such as a lawyer, a doctor or a teacher. Of course, being a magician myself I often see it as a magician! However, it can also represent trickery or deception, depending on what other cards are beside it or the situation the client is in at the time of the reading.

Now, this should be pretty easy to remember because a magician uses tricks to deceive you! However, if you think of the magician as a 'wonder worker' whenever you see this card, it will bring to mind someone who is pretty efficient and has the ability to solve problems. That of course will bring to mind a professional person such as I have described.

2. The High Priestess

To me this represents a very wise woman who is quite spiritual. A kind person in fact. Someone who gives good advice.

To remember this, just associate this card in your mind to someone you know who fits that description. It could be your mother, your wife or in fact anyone you know who is worldly wise. Once you have that image in your mind, it will be easy to remember. Sometimes the card represents to me a guardian angel of some kind. Again, a lot depends on the circumstances of the reading and the neighboring cards. Of course, guardian angels tend to evoke spiritual images, so the very phrase "High Priestess" will bring this interpretation to mind straight away.

3. The Empress

I think of this card as a very efficient woman. Well organized, with a strong personality. Possibly even a businesswoman. Someone financially secure.

One aid to remember this meaning is to follow the same procedure I suggested for the High Priestess card. In other words, think of someone you know who fits at least part of the above description. I tend to think of Margaret Thatcher, the former British prime minister!

4. The Emperor

A businessman perhaps, or someone with a strong personality. Someone in authority. Possibly wealthy with a lot of leadership qualities. Basically, the same as the Empress but a male rather than a female!

Again, think of someone you know who fits that description to some degree, and this card's meaning will stick in your memory.

5. The Hierophant

In most Tarot decks, the Hierophant card shows a picture of the Pope. This should bring to mind religious matters, or perhaps someone who is either very spiritual or very religious. It can bring to mind the picture of a church, which in turn can bring to mind the picture of people marrying in a church. In other words, it can be a marriage card. Sometimes it means to me a guardian angel, just as it does with the High Priestess card.

As you can now see, it is very easy to memorize this card very quickly just by looking at the Pope. And you don't even have to be Catholic to do it!

6. The Lovers

This obviously represents love and won't be hard to remember! However, although the card is self-explanatory, it can also mean love in a general sense, such as friends and family.

7. The Chariot

To me, this card represents victory after a struggle. I will give you the little script that I sometimes use with a client when this card shows up. The script itself will help you remember the card.

"This card means victory after a struggle. You see how he is trying to control the two horses? A black horse and a white horse. The black horse is going one way, the white horse is going the other way. He is having a struggle getting the two horses under control. But he does get them under control! He emerges victorious after a struggle. And you will also emerge victorious after a struggle. You will get there in the end. It might be tough going but you will get there."

8. Strength

This is virtually self-explanatory. It can mean strength of character, strength in facing obstacles, determination, resilience and so on. In other words, the client will have the inner strength to overcome difficulties.

9. The Hermit

To me, this card represents someone who needs a bit of space on their own. They don't want to be too crowded in. Someone who needs time to reflect, meditate or make decisions on their own. It can often represent studying, since people often study on their own.

Sometimes I will interpret the card as meaning that the client has to proceed slowly and not rush into things. I base this on the image of the Hermit holding a lamp in front of him so he can see where he is going. Just looking at this card should bring the above possibilities to mind and make the card easy enough to remember.

10. Wheel of Fortune

This should be an easy card to remember, since to me it means the wheel of fortune is about to turn in the client's favor. It is really a card of good luck. Again, this card is virtually self-explanatory and won't need much memorizing.

11. Justice

Whenever I see this card it reminds me of possible legal matters coming up. I tell the client that a legal matter doesn't have to be a court case. It can also represent signing a document or a contract.

Sometimes I will interpret it as a decision that has to be made. This is triggered by the image of the scales being held in the picture. Again, this should be pretty easy to remember.

12. The Hanged Man

To me, this card represents sacrifice. To be honest, I can't remember exactly why I decided it meant this. However, it is a picture of a man hanging upside down, and I suppose that is indeed a bit of a sacrifice! Another Tarot reader once told me that it represented, to her, truth, because truth was often upside down! I suppose you could also say that it represents the client's life being a bit upside down at the moment and needs to be sorted out.

Anyway, these are just a few suggestions. Whichever you choose will be easy to associate with the image of the poor chap hanging upside down and be very easy to remember!

13. Death

This can be a scary card to people, but it doesn't actually mean physical death. In fact, to me it can be quite a good card. It means change. Transformation. Death of the old, beginning of the new. The end of one cycle in life and the start of another. For example, if someone is going to emigrate, they can easily get the death card. If they are about to start a new job, they can get it, too. If someone is about to get married, they can get the death card. Mind you, if they are about to get divorced, they can also get the death card!

Anyway, remembering the card it is pretty easy. Whenever you see it, just think, "The death of the old and the beginning of the new."

14. Temperance

Again, pretty self-explanatory. This means just what it says. Temperance in all areas. Don't drink too much, don't smoke too much and don't worry too much. Oh, and don't gamble—that can be a bad one!

15. The Devil

This should be easy to remember, since the Devil represents temptation. Somewhat similar to the Temperance card, but not quite. It can mean sexual temptation for example. I find that it often shows the client is a good spender. They see something they like, buy it first and worry about the consequences afterwards. Probably the reason they are paying you for a reading, I suppose, so you had better not complain about it!

I find the card can often represent anger and a tendency to lose one's temper.

16. The Tower

I see this as the worst card in the pack. This alone makes it easy to remember! The image shows thunder, lightning, and people falling out of the tower! In some versions of the Tarot, you can actually see the tower falling apart! It can be interpreted as all sorts of disasters about to befall the Querent, but I think it very unwise to say stuff like this to a client, especially a very vulnerable person, as it can scare them badly and set up a self-fulfilling prophecy.

I far prefer to play things down and interpret the card as some confusion or worrisome situation, but I always predict that these problems will be overcome. Very often the client will already be aware of these situations and will be pleased to hear that they will be resolved in the end.

I will also on occasion interpret the card as obstacles in the path to success, but will balance this by pointing to a more positive card in the spread, such as the Sun Card, Star Card or the Wheel of Fortune, and say that they indicate that the obstacles will be overcome. If there are no positive cards in the spread, I will say it anyway! That is what I mean by "streetwise" Tarot! I see no point in upsetting people unduly.

On the other hand, it is not good policy to make a reading a complete bed of roses and simply tell the client what they want to hear. After all, life is not like that, and if you make things too bright and wonderful, the client may tend not to believe you. Therefore, my policy is to keep things mostly positive in a reading but also to include some *mild* negativity to balance things out a little and maintain credibility.

17. The Star

This is my favorite card. I consider it the second-best card in the pack. (The best one is the Sun card, which I will come to later.) It means that the client's wish is very likely to come true. To remember this easily, just think of the well-known phrase, "wishing on a star". However, I do have to temper this a trifle, in case what the client is wishing for is a bit on the impossible side, and I would not want them to be hurt or upset in the future if the wish doesn't come true.

You can do a lot of good for people, but you can also do a lot of harm if you are not careful, and I will discuss this later in the chapter on ethics. I therefore temper things a little by saying, "Your wish is likely to come true. However, it may come true in a slightly different way than you expect, but there is always a positive result from this card. Sometimes what appears to be negative turns out to be positive—you know—blessings in disguise".

18. The Moon

The Moon is generally not a good card. It shows a certain amount of stress and worry that is present. Ambitions that seem to be hard to fulfill. Not getting the things wanted. It's a little trickier to remember this one, since the design on the Moon card varies from one deck to another. One deck I use is the hard-to-obtain Prediction deck. The Moon card in that deck does indeed show a very dark and dreary background and a rather miserable moon figure, which would indeed remind you of stress and worry. However, as I indicated, this deck is out of production and hard to obtain.

The much more available Rider-Waite deck shows a much brighter Moon card that doesn't give quite the same impression. However, it shows a couple of dogs howling at the moon, which can show irritation. It always reminds me of unfulfilled ambitions.

One obvious memory aid is to think of a full moon. You probably know this is supposed to cause change of moods. Some experts say that it means moodiness and depression.

When the card shows up, I always try to find other, more positive cards in the spread to show that the worries will ease. Mind you, I have to concede that other authorities say a full moon means good luck! The streetwise approach is to say that it means stress and worry, so let us not get too "stressed" out and "worried" about what it really means! After all, as already explained, *you* decide what the cards mean, not some esoteric spirit guide or mystical force of the universe! By all means, have a different meaning than the one I am indicating here, as long as it is a reasonable meaning and easy to remember. I am giving you guidelines and nothing more.

19. The Sun

Most Tarot readers, including myself, consider this to be the best card in the pack. It means good fortune and success is ahead for the client. Happiness in all areas such as love, health, work and money.

This should be easy to remember, since the Sun tends to make all of us feel happy (unless we get sunburn, of course!).

The Major Arcana

20. Judgement

This card represents to me that a decision has to be made. I tell the client that only he or she can make the decision and that no Tarot reader can make it on their behalf. I do mention that, once they make their mind up after careful thought, they should go ahead without fear. In fact, sometimes making the wrong decision is better than no decision at all.

The card is easy to remember, since all you have to do is remember that, when a person makes a decision, they have to use good judgement.

21. The World

This is almost self-explanatory since, to me, the World card represents travel or movement. Obviously, when I see the card, travel comes to mind immediately. It can either mean travelling to see someone or that someone comes to see the client. Of course, it can also mean travelling on business or for pleasure, depending on what other cards show up in the spread. Sometimes I find that it means moving house, too.

22. The Fool

The Fool card does not necessarily mean foolishness, although it usually does. Again, a lot depends on which deck you are using. In the Prediction deck already mentioned, it shows someone trying to make their mind up and a lot of indecision going on. In the more commonly used Rider-Waite deck, it shows a man not looking where he is going and about to walk over a cliff! I suppose that does represent a certain foolishness! However, the chap seems to show a very cheerful and adventurous nature, so that tends to represent to me a very optimistic outlook on life, although perhaps a little too optimistic in this particular case!

I do tend not to inform the client that the card represents foolishness, even though it actually does! After all, it might not be the most tactful of approaches!

In any event I think there is enough information here to make the card easy to remember.

OK. Those are the 22 cards of the Major Arcana out of the way. The next chapter will deal with the Minor Arcana.

CHAPTER THREE
The Minor Arcana

The Minor Arcana consists of fifty-six cards, which, at first sight, may seem a much bigger challenge to remember than the Major Arcana. However, this is not necessarily so. Again, a lot depends on which deck you are using. The deck I am recommending for beginners is the Rider-Waite deck, as this particular pack has a picture on every card in the deck. However, many other brands of the Tarot only have pictures on the Major Arcana. This means that I will have to present to you two different options with regard to remembering the meanings. Actually three, but I will come to that later.

For the purpose of this chapter, I am only going to deal with forty cards of the Minor Arcana, since the remaining sixteen cards represent people. These are called court cards. There are four Page cards, four Knights, four Queens and four Kings. I shall leave those aside for the moment and deal with them in the next chapter to avoid confusion. The other reason is that I can then have seven chapters in this book instead of six! That is because seven is a spiritual number and I think it will bring this book good luck!

With the Rider-Waite deck, the best option, as I have already explained elsewhere, is to go through the deck in private and decide what each card means to you just by looking at the pictures and seeing what you can come up with.

For example, I have a deck of Rider-Waite Tarot cards in front of me as I write. What I will do right now is to spread the cards in a row face down and choose any three cards at random, but discarding any Major Arcana cards that show up, as they are not relevant in this discussion. If one does show up, I will simply discard it and remove another card in its stead.

The first card I picked is the Judgement card of the Major Arcana, so I shall ignore that and start again. Now I have the Hierophant, so it seems the Major Arcana does not want to leave me alone! I shall try again! Oh no! The Death card! This probably means my search will soon be coming to an end. Hopefully by the time I get to the end of this book! Uh oh, now I have the Queen of Wands, which is relevant for the next chapter, but not right now! I think I will try one more card and if it doesn't fit, I may abandon this whole exercise. Oh no! The Emperor card!

I am being plagued by a lot of irrelevant cards, mostly Major Arcana ones. I have often thought that the Major Arcana are the most powerful cards in the Tarot deck and this little exercise seems to have proven it to be the case.

I think a better procedure may be for me to remove all the Pages, Knights, Queens, Kings, and the Major Arcana, and start again. It should save me a lot of typing at any rate!

OK. I have sorted out the cards and am about to try again.

All right. I now have three cards of the Minor Arcana right in front of me: the Two of Coins, the Seven of Swords and the Ten of Wands. Let us take the Two of Coins first. It shows a picture of a man who seems to be juggling two large coins. This could well represent the client having trouble making ends meet. Perhaps spending more money than he or she should.

Now the Seven of Swords. The picture shows a man carrying a whole bunch of swords. To me, it looks like someone gathering up weapons after a battle. I could therefore interpret that as the client has faced a battle, but now the battle is over and he or she doesn't have to worry about it anymore. Of course, that would be *my* interpretation rather than yours. What you may see in the picture could well be different from what I see. By all means, use your own interpretation and your own imagination to form your own meaning to what you see in the picture. It will be more memorable that way.

Finally, we have the Ten of Wands. It shows a picture of someone carrying a lot of heavy sticks. To me this looks like someone who works very hard, possibly too hard, and of course this may apply to the client as well.

Anyway, this should give you a bit of an idea what I am getting at. Look at each card of the Minor Arcana, meditate on it and figure out what it means to YOU according to the picture you see. Before you know it, you will remember the meanings of all forty cards of the Minor Arcana, except of course for the court cards, which will be dealt with in the next chapter.

The Minor Arcana

That is one method of learning the Minor Arcana. However, as I have already mentioned, not every deck has a picture on every card in the same way that the Rider-Waite deck and all its variants have. There are many Tarot decks where the Minor Arcana have no pictures or images to help you. In fact, the very first deck I ever used, the aforementioned Prediction deck, has no images on the Minor Arcana.

So, what do you do? How do you remember forty different cards when there are no images to help you? Actually, it is not that hard once you realize that there are only ten cards to remember, rather than forty! Let me explain. First, I will deal with the suits, which are Wands (sometimes known as Staves), Swords, Cups, and Pentacles (sometimes known as Coins). These are equivalent to clubs, spades, hearts and diamonds in a regular deck of playing cards.

These are the meanings of the suits:

1. Wands

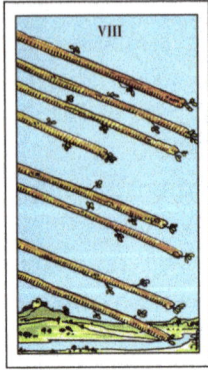  

This is a bit tricky, since my research indicates that different authorities on the Tarot seem to have different opinions on what this means! That can create confusion! However, the good news is that this confusion can be easy to remember if you simply ascribe the word "confusion" to the suit! To me, Wands represent worry and confusion. The "confusion" means that nobody seems to know what the hell Wands means and the "worry" bit means the best thing to do is not "worry" about it!

Not very spiritual, I know, but I did say this was the "streetwise" method of learning the Tarot!

Having said all the above, I will concede that sometimes I ascribe health matters to the Wand suit. I suppose one way of remembering this is to realize that if you bonk someone over the head with a heavy wand, it would not be very good for their health!

One other Tarot authority friend of mine believes that Wands mean social activities, and his memory suggestion was to imagine waving a magic wand to bring all your friends together! By all means use this meaning and image if you want. As I keep mentioning, there are no strict rules as to how you read the Tarot.

The Minor Arcana

2. Swords

Alas, this suit is another one where there seems to be disagreement on which meaning is correct! I have often thought that different Tarot card readers end up doing things differently according to which Tarot book they read when they first started!

To my great amusement, one Tarot author wrote two books on the subject and each book had a different meaning for the Swords suit!

I, personally, have several meanings for Swords, depending on which cards show up in a reading, but I better not tell you what they are, otherwise you will get completely confused and wish you hadn't started!

A lot of Tarot readers ascribe Swords to conflict. That, of course, is easy to remember, because all you have to do is think of swords crossing.

One reader I know believes that Swords represents business. He suggests you imagine picking up a sword to defend your business.

To me, generally speaking, Swords means work, career, and your occupation in general. I suppose the best way to remember this is to imagine fighting for a living, which of course, most of us have to do in this modern world. And of course, Swords will remind you of fighting.

I think some readers ascribe a very negative meaning to the Swords suit. The reason I say this, apart from the fact that some Tarot books I have read do seem to put a negative slant on this suit, is that on several occasions, when I have a client in front of me, there is a sharp intake of breath when they see this suit showing up, and they will say something like, "Oh, Swords! That must be bad news," and of course I have to explain to him or her (usually her!) that Swords do not necessarily mean bad news at all.

I really dislike this particular meaning, since, after all, there are fourteen Sword cards in the deck, and it is inevitable that a few are going to be selected and show up in the spread. I like my readings to be generally positive and I want people at the end of the reading to be feeling happy rather than miserable! I think there is enough misery in the world without adding any more through the Tarot, don't you?

3. Cups

This suit is a lot easier to deal with, since most Tarot authorities generally agree that it means love, either of family, friends, romantic love, love of work, hobby or activity. Perhaps simply even love of life. Just think of the "cup of love" and the meaning of the suit will come to you automatically.

4. Pentacles (Coins)

This is also an easy one, since, as indicated above, Pentacles is really just another word for Coins. Well, it isn't, really, but for our purposes, it is, since in Tarot images they look like coins anyway. I can also say that in some Tarot decks, the word "Pentacles" is used, and in some other decks, the word "Coins" is used.

The Minor Arcana

Now, most Tarot readers equate Pentacle cards with business, finance, material possessions and money matters generally. Therefore, just looking at what appears to be big gold coins in the images will certainly bring the meaning of the suit to mind immediately.

Now that we have gotten the suits out of the way, let me deal with the numbers. You will remember that earlier, I stated that you only have to learn ten meanings rather than forty. That is because each number has the same meaning for the four suits, only in different spheres of life. For example, the Ace means a new beginning, a new opportunity, or a new cycle in life. The Two represents a partnership of some kind. The Three represents obstacles to be overcome.

Now, think about it. Once you know the suit, all you have to do is to learn the meaning for each card and apply it to that suit.

Let us take the Ace, for example. I have stated that it represents new opportunities. That means that the Ace of Swords can represent a new job, the Ace of Cups a new relationship, the Ace of Coins a new financial opportunity, and the Ace of Wands something new to worry about! With regard to the last one, I don't like to create new burdens for people, so I would tend to say the opposite meaning and imply the client's worries are about to come to an end! That is the "streetwise" way of going about things, after all!

The same kind of procedure goes for the Two. Two of Cups can mean a relationship. Two of Pentacles can mean a partnership in business. Get the idea? Same for the number Three, which means obstacles. Well, you can have obstacles in love, work, business and, in fact, virtually every sphere of your life.

You can deduce from all the above that you really only have to learn the meanings of ten numbers and four suits. Ten times four is forty! So, in other words, you only really have to learn ten cards rather than forty!

Luckily there are memory tricks to remember the ten numbers. Here we go.

ACE

Aces also represent the number one. Aces are beginnings, just like number one. Think of counting from one to ten. You start at one, the beginning!

TWO
Self-explanatory. It means a partnership. Just think "two of a kind".

THREE
I have already explained that this means obstacles to be overcome. The way you remember this is to think of "two's company, three's a crowd".

However, I must say that, quite frankly, I don't like this particular "obstacles" meaning, because it will be repeated for the number eight when we get to it. I would tend to find another meaning for the number three. As will shortly be explained, I personally use a numerology system for my number meanings, and the meaning for three in numerology is creativity. The trouble is that I am not sure what memory trick can be used for that word. That means I will have to use my creativity to figure it out.

Oh! I just did! When you see the number three, just think that you will have to be creative to figure out a meaning for it and you will have it! And of course, you have to be creative in work, money, love and, in fact, every facet of your life.

FOUR
This means building foundations. If you think of the four cornerstones which act as the foundations of a house or building, it will bring the meaning to mind.

FIVE
This represents difficulties. So, to remember this, all you have to do is visualize how difficult it is to draw a five-pointed star.

SIX
This number represents success. All you have to do is remember you are playing a dice game. The highest number you can get is six when you play dice. That means success! Easy enough to remember!

SEVEN
This means lessons to learn. Imagine when you first go to kindergarten at the age of five but didn't start to take lessons until the age of seven. Before that time it was mostly play. That should bring the meaning to mind.

EIGHT
As I mentioned previously, this number represents obstacles to be overcome. Just imagine an obstacle course laid out like a figure eight, where you finish up back where you started, and the meaning will come to mind.

NINE
This number means achievements. If you think of getting nine out of ten, that is a pretty good achievement. Easy to remember!

TEN
This number represents final outcomes. All you have to do here is imagine a boxer being knocked out for the count. When the referee counts up to ten, that is the final outcome.

Phew! Now that the above is out of the way, I shall remind you that, at the beginning of this chapter, I mentioned there are three ways of remembering the Minor Arcana. Well, I am going to explain the third option now.

It is actually the option I use myself. It is somewhat similar to the option I just outlined above using memory tricks, and applies to decks that have no pictures or images on the Minor Arcana. However, the main difference is that the meanings I use for the numbers are mostly different than the meanings already described in the preceding explanation. They are based on regular numerology.

Furthermore, I have no memory aids to suggest, although there may well be some that I don't know about or have no time to invent right now. Still, there are only ten groups of suggested meanings, so it shouldn't be too much of a burden. As for the meanings of the suits in my system, it is more or less the same as I have already described, so at least we won't have to worry about that.

Here are the meanings that I personally use for the numbers. Just a few key words but you can expand on them to your heart's content.

ONE
Independence. New beginnings. Offers, propositions or suggestions.

TWO
Relationships. Contracts. Agreements. Conflicts.

THREE
This is a light-hearted number to me. It means creativity, joy, laughter, celebration.

FOUR
Hard work. Stubbornness. Resilience. Energy and stamina. Organizational ability.

FIVE
Travel. Freedom and variety. Dislike of restriction. Change.

SIX
This is the number of home and family, particularly children. Love. It is also a number of the intellect.

SEVEN
To me this represents spirituality. Needing time to be on one's own. Studying and learning. Sometimes learning the hard way. Meditating.

EIGHT
This is the money number. Anything to do with business or finances. It can also mean good health and long life. Energy. Hard work. Stubbornness.

NINE
Compassion. Humanity. Finishing what one starts. Things coming to an end.

TEN
I don't really have a numerology meaning for this one. I simply use the same definition as in the last method. In other words, final outcomes. You can use the same memory trick of the boxer being knocked out for the count.

This brings me to an important point. There is absolutely no reason that you can't mix and match the various systems. I often overlap things when I do readings. For example, if I see a card in a spread that fits a situation better than my numerology reading, I won't hesitate to use one of the memory trick meanings instead. Sometimes I even do this with the Rider-Waite deck, even though the image on the cards has nothing to do with, say, the numerology meaning. I do what fits, and with all three systems, you have the flexibility to do it.

By all means, for now, choose one of the three systems explained and stick to it until you get more experience. However, as time goes by, you will find that having all three systems at your disposal can be very useful indeed.

For example, if I have a repeat client that I have seen many times before, in order that I don't find myself repeating the same words and phrases, I will switch decks from the Prediction Deck, which has no images on the Minor Arcana, to the Rider-Waite, which does. I can then interpret the cards according to the images, just as in the first method I described in this chapter. The truth of the matter is that there are no rules set in stone with the Tarot. Especially the streetwise method of reading the Tarot!

One other point. Many traditional Tarot readers use reversed card meanings. That is, if a card is the right way up, you have one meaning. If it is upside down, it means the opposite. This, of course, means you have to learn twice as many meanings! I feel that the infinite combinations of cards and meanings shown in a spread are more than sufficient to do an excellent reading, so I do not use reversed card meanings. Enough is enough, I think, and I can assure you that I am not the only Tarot practitioner who feels this way. Tradition or not, many excellent readers eschew the reversed card meanings. Again, it is the streetwise thing to do and will save you a lot of extra work having to learn twice as many meanings!

OK. At this point I have covered the meanings of all of the cards except for the court cards. I will deal with them in the next chapter. Onwards....

CHAPTER FOUR
The Court Cards

There are sixteen cards to learn and memorize here: the four Pages, the four Knights, the four Queens and the four Kings. Now, although I said sixteen cards, in actual practice, there are only four to remember! That is because, just as has been previously explained in connection with the number cards in the Minor Arcana, all the Pages, Knights, Queens and Kings have the same meanings but in different spheres.

1. Queens

For example, let us take the Queen. It represents a woman and, of course, that won't take much in the way of memory work! However, because of the four suits, it can represent four kinds of women! Thus, if we take, for example, the Queen of Pentacles (Coins), this could represent a woman who is good at business or perhaps careful with money. Of course, you might prefer the opposite meaning and consider it to be a woman who spends money like water! I personally make it mean either, depending on what other cards are beside it, or alternatively, whatever mood I am in at the time of the reading! After all, the streetwise approach to reading Tarot is that nothing is cast in tablets of stone. You do what works. You could also say that the Queen of Pentacles shows a woman who loves money and jewelry. Perhaps she is a businesswoman.

The point I am trying to make is that, though the meaning of any of the Queen cards is of a woman, you define the meaning more specifically by the suit. Thus, the Queen of Pentacles (Coins) can represent all or any of the meanings described, but the Queen of Cups could represent a woman who is emotional and loving. The Queen of Swords could represent a woman who is always busy and not afraid of hard work, whereas the Queen of Wands could be a woman who worries too much. However, all four cards represent a woman of some kind.

2. Knights and Kings

The same thing applies to the four Knights and Kings. The Knights represent younger men and the Kings older men. Easy to remember. They follow exactly the same pattern as the Queens with regard to fine tuning the type of man represented by the suit.

3. Pages

The Pages represent children. Just think of a pageboy and this meaning will come to mind. I won't go through the meanings of each Page, since it will be better for you to exercise your own imagination and creativity in this regard, but here is a quick example to act as a guideline. Take the Page of Pentacles (Coins). This can represent a child who will have the potential to make money in life as he grows older.

Sometimes I use the Page card to represent new opportunities and challenges in life. Thus, the Page of Swords can represent a new job offer or promotion to me.

You have to let your imagination and creativity run a little wild here when interpreting the cards, combined with your intuitive—and sometimes not so intuitive—assessment of the client. Still, I will delve into that more when we get to the interpretation chapter a little later on.

Right now, I think our next chapter may well be the most important chapter in this entire book: the ethics involved in doing Tarot readings. I don't see this mentioned much in other books on the Tarot. Well, better late than never! Turn the page and let's get on with it!

CHAPTER FIVE
Ethics

This is a very difficult subject that does not really seem to be discussed much in books on the Tarot. It is true that I consider Tarot cards to be the most powerful divination tool known to man, but it is also true that dynamite is pretty powerful too, and you can get blown up by it if you are not careful! Of course, it is unlikely that you will blow a client up during a reading—I have often blown a client away with my accuracy, but have never blown them up! However, although you may not destroy your client physically, if you say the wrong thing during a reading, you can destroy that person psychologically.

Many Tarot card readers are sincere, compassionate people who really believe in their work and try to help their clients as best they can. However, some of them are hampered by too much belief, which I believe can be detrimental. Words are like the dynamite I referred to before. An overly confident feeling by a Tarot reader that his or her interpretation is the correct one can result in faulty predictions and advice, which can be unintentionally harmful. As the old saying goes, "The road to hell is paved with good intentions."

This is the advantage of the streetwise approach. Someone who is streetwise and very experienced in life's ups and downs is far more likely to be aware of the right thing to say during a reading than someone who means well but is innocent in the ways of this wicked world we all live in. Enthusiastic faith in the Tarot is one thing; naivety is another.

I believe that life can be likened to a game of snakes and ladders. A streetwise reader can use the Tarot to help navigate the path so that the client can avoid the snakes and climb the ladders.

As a reader, you are walking a minefield, an ethical tight rope. You can do so much good, but if you are not careful, you can also do so much harm. The bit that frightens me is not deliberate harm. I would never do that and I would assume that you won't either. The main problem that should terrify the living daylights out of a Tarot reader is doing accidental harm to someone, by what he or she says.

What happens if the reader influences someone the wrong way? A well-meaning reader may wish to give advice, but what happens if he or she gives the wrong advice? What happens if the reader's prejudices enter into a reading, and his or her own values predominate?

Even a simple thing like a daily horoscope in a newspaper can be problematic. It can possibly influence someone to do something stupid if they take it too seriously. What happens if the newspaper horoscope says that it's not a good day to travel? Is it possible that a person doesn't travel based on that information and loses out on an important business deal? Most people will not be affected. Some will not take it seriously, but you can bet that some will and will lose out in some way.

You may say that the astrologer cannot be held responsible if someone overreacts. But he or she wrote the horoscope that influenced the event, so how responsible is that person?

In my Tarot practice I try to predict positive outcomes rather than negative ones. The problem arises that I don't know everything, and although my predictions tend to be very accurate indeed, I have to confess—reluctantly—that I am not quite as perfect as I like to think I am! That means, in a minority of occasions, my positive outlook on events in a person's life doesn't necessarily work out. That creates the unfortunate possibility that the client is going to be more disappointed than if I had just kept my mouth shut in the first place. False hope can be worse than no hope at all.

I do have to sleep at night, so in order to placate my uneasy conscience over this issue, my solution to the problem is twofold. First, I always inform the client before I lay the cards out that a Tarot reading is a bit like a weather forecast. I explain that a weather forecaster may predict that it is going to rain next week, and of course, it usually does, in the same way my Tarot predictions usually work out. However, I also explain that there are bound to be occasions when the forecaster gets things wrong—and of course I can get things wrong too.

The other thing I do is to give out a promotional flyer with every reading. It serves two purposes. The first is—naturally—to promote my services! However, in addition to telling the client how wonderful I am, it gives me a chance to issue the disclaimer below. It not only allows me to anaesthetise my conscience somewhat, it also could prove useful in the unlikely event that, one day, I may wish to work in a jurisdiction where fortune telling and kindred activities can run into legal difficulties. In those cases, the phrase "For Entertainment Only" is usually a good safeguard in these matters.

> ### DISCLAIMER
>
> A psychic reading can be a very powerful experience. Tarot cards in particular offer guidance and insight. However, I always emphasise to my clients that nothing is cast in tablets of stone. YOU have the power to alter your own life. We all have free will and your destiny CAN be altered no matter what any psychic says. Predictions, therefore, cannot be guaranteed any more than a weather forecast always comes out as expected. My own predictions have a high rate of accuracy but I cannot claim absolute perfection. I don't see everything and neither would I want to. I refuse to play God. For this reason, ALL READINGS ARE FOR FUN AND ENTERTAINMENT ONLY. Please use YOUR OWN COMMON SENSE when evaluating the information you receive.

However, for those of my readers who are of a more metaphysical frame of mind and who might prefer a more airy-fairy mystical disclaimer, this might fit the bill:

> ### IMPORTANT NOTICE
>
> Any advice or counsel received fits into the parameters of Self-Help and Personal or Spiritual Growth. Consequently, the payment made to the consultant during this time is for services rendered in this context only.
>
> It is accepted that the individual's free will can influence the course of events that will occur in life, as these events are not unchangeable. Knowing this gives the ability, to a certain degree, to control the future. Time is a continuum and the past/present/future is no more than a perception of a perpetual movement. There is no future as such in the usual meaning of the consultant's discourse; there are only probabilities, trends and projections based on the past and present.
>
> Consequently, the consultant makes no public claim to foretell, foresee or predict the future. In forecasting events, readings may be interpreted for fun and entertainment purposes only.

Now, I don't claim to have all the answers to these ethical conundrums, but I do believe that at least you have to be aware of the question in order to work out your own answer and help you sleep at night, to satisfy your conscience.

One way to avoid the issue is to become like a crooked psychic reader, of whom there are regrettably a great many. They have no conscience whatsoever regarding the clients they see. They are terrible people who would probably sell their children if business was a bit slow! They are TOO streetwise! They will pull stunts such as saying there is a curse on the client (there isn't!) and demand exorbitant sums of money to remove the curse, which doesn't exist in the first place!

I still remember one of my clients who was in a vulnerable state, telling me about the time she went to consult with one of these bloodsuckers. The usual baloney was offered concerning a curse, and she was told that, in order to remove the dreaded jinx, it would be necessary for the "psychic" to travel to Jerusalem to obtain special candles, and of course that would be very expensive and she would need to be compensated for her time and travel costs. I doubt she even went to her local corner store to pick up said mysterious candles!

I have heard horror story after horror story concerning these vicious con artists. Unbelievable sums of money can be extorted from vulnerable people over a period, running into many, many thousands of dollars. When the client runs out of money, the crooked psychic hasn't necessarily finished. The client may be asked to donate valuable personal property, such as jewellery, instead as payment.

You may wonder how intelligent people would fall for such things, but clients are often vulnerable and desperate when they see a reader and can be easily deceived because they are not thinking straight. Furthermore, the crooked Tarot reader will advise the client not to tell a soul about the reading, otherwise the curse will return! That, of course, is because the client is liable to be persuaded by their friends that there is deception going on!

These scam artists, for some reason, are not prosecuted very often, possibly because the authorities have higher priorities, and cases are either not reported or difficult to prove.

However, it is pretty easy to spot crooked Tarot readers by their advertising. They use a lot of phrases that are dead giveaways, such as "reunites lost lovers," "removes curses," "black magic," "99% accurate," and other stock phrases. Incidentally, if you see a reader using

Ethics

the word "enemies" in their advertising, run a mile. The REAL enemy is the reader herself!

I suppose one advantage of going this route is that you don't have to worry about ethics. The disadvantage is that karma will catch up with you and evil will bounce back on you in the long run. It always does.

However, some honest readers can do just as much harm. They may not scam the client financially but can do so psychologically. They can misinterpret things and feel that they *have* to convey that misinterpretation to the client. If they see something negative, they feel that it is their duty to inform the client of the disaster that is about to befall them. It's the height of stupidity for two reasons. One is that the imagined event probably isn't going to happen anyway, and secondly, even if it is, what is the point of scaring people unnecessarily?

It is true that I sometimes see a negative event that is likely to happen to a client, but I also know that nothing is cast in tablets of stone and that it is perfectly possible to alter a negative path and avoid the unpleasant event. I will indeed give advice on this if I deem it necessary. However, this is a far cry from telling someone they are going to contract a serious illness, have an accident or die at a certain age, as some sincere but rather daft readers do.

They will justify this dangerous nonsense by saying they feel that they have to tell the client everything they see, either bad or good. The client will often encourage this nonsense by saying, "I want to know all the bad things you see." Quite frankly, my response to this is, "Of course. I will tell you everything I see, whether bad or good," but then of course I ignore what I just said to them and make the reading as positive as possible!

I may well include some mild negativity to make the reading credible and give good advice at the same time, but I see no point in predicting gloom and doom because of some imaginary disaster that I might see in the cards. That is the "streetwise" approach!

There is such a thing as a self-fulfilling prophecy. A reader can plant a seed by making a prediction. That seed can grow and develop over time within the subconscious mind of the client, which somehow does all it can to make the prediction come true, and it often will because of that. Now, the Tarot reader has a choice as to whether to plant a negative seed or a positive one. It seems common sense to me to plant a positive seed rather than a negative one. In other words, try to be a good gardener!

I do remember when I first started that I was not a good gardener. This sad tale took place around thirty-three years ago and hopefully, it will be a warning to some of my less experienced readers. I predicted to one woman she would meet a man with dark hair, have the initial P, and she would develop a warm, loving relationship with him. Maybe I got a psychic vibe about it, but in retrospect I think it was more likely a trick of my imagination and I managed to fool myself.

Remember the self-fulfilling prophecy? She did meet the man with the dark hair, he did have the initial P. Good, wasn't it?

No, it wasn't. The relationship was a disaster. How guilty did I feel when I heard about it? To be honest, only a little. But then I heard that she stuck with him longer than she should have done, because I predicted that it would work out. She tried to make the self-fulfilling prophecy work, against her own common sense.

How guilty did I feel then? Quite a lot, actually. I never give initials or descriptions of people now, put it that way.

I suppose I am issuing a warning to my readers not to make the same mistakes that I have made in my long career. I've done thousands of readings and I know that I've done much, much good. But I don't know if I can put my hand on my heart and be 100% sure that amongst those thousands of readings, I have not misguided someone and spoiled the quality of their life in some way. Now, I'm not saying I have, but I can't be sure that I haven't ruined someone's life with some stupidity I may have uttered. I don't think I have. I pray that I haven't. But I don't *know* that I haven't.

Of course, I could rationalise and say things like, "Well, even doctors and psychiatrists make occasional mistakes, and my batting average is probably better than theirs." But do two wrongs make a right?

I suppose I could rationalise even further and say that 80% of the people that come to me get benefit. The people who suffer from the reading have to pay the price for the ones who profit. A sacrifice for the greater good? I wonder.

Now, I'm not saying that I have all the answers to these issues, or that any answers I do have apply to you. All I'm saying is you should be aware of the minefield you're entering and ask your own questions. You ultimately will have to form your own ethical position and be responsible for your own decisions. I have formed mine and my readings are fraught with less difficulty as I have become more experienced.

Now, the problem is that you are using human guinea pigs while you get experience. I try not to think of the blunders I made when I first started. I can console myself that I have never tried to deliberately make anyone unhappy. But are good intentions enough? Now, the world is full of well-intentioned people who do great harm. I bet my readers can think of examples of this in their own experience.

You may not mean to cause harm as a Tarot reader, but can you be sure that you won't? Now, excuse me for all this agonising in print, but if you're going to deal with people's lives, you'd better figure out your own ethical stance and feel as comfortable as you can with it.

You'll have to make your own decisions on this. If you have, after all this, still decided that the Tarot-reading route is the one you would like to pursue, I can give you some suggestions that will make the ethical part less of a burden—and it should be a burden. If it's not a burden for you, I suspect you should give up the Tarot, for the sake of your clients.

Suggestion Number One:
Never give medical or legal advice. Be ready to refer them to a doctor, lawyer or financial counsellor.

If they ask about health in a general way and they look OK to me, I'll say to them: "Have you ever heard the old saying, 'No news is good news?' I am not picking up any bad health vibrations around you, but I always tell people that if you ever feel sick, see a doctor, not a Tarot reader!" and then I smile. Now they always smile too in response, since they always realise how ridiculous it is to see a psychic about health.

The same thing applies to legal matters or financial difficulties. I tell them that they need to discuss these matters with a lawyer or financial counsellor. I think it's all right to predict a favourable outcome to the matter if you sense it and the cards show it, but always refer them to a professional.

Suggestion Number Two
Payment

There are, of course, ethical issues to be raised over the fees you may decide to charge for a reading. Obviously, Tarot readers should be paid for their services. Or at least they should be once they have gained sufficiency in experience and know what they are doing. The problem with unpaid readings is that the client will tend to put a nothing value on them. It is OK to do free readings for people while you are gaining experience and learning your trade, but once you have gained proficiency, then it is time to start charging real money.

That is because payment is part of the therapy. The point I am trying to make is that the client will not value the guidance you give him or her if they don't pay a reasonable price for the service you offer. If you get something for nothing, there is a tendency to put a nothing value on it. That's why people pay higher prices for certain items; not necessarily that the item is of better quality, but because they imagine the item is better quality.

Never feel guilty about charging a reasonable fee for your reading. Counsellors of all kind get paid and so should you. Doctors, psychiatrists, and social workers all get paid. Financial counsellors always make sure their own financial needs take priority over their own clients's. I can assure you of that! Their fees are in the same league as Tarot readers, and I suspect higher! As for doctors and clergy, they all get paid, too!

People will not get the full benefit from a session if they do not pay a reasonable fee. They'll feel better and be more believing in you if they have paid to believe in you. Of course, you do have to give value for money and make sure you give an excellent reading.

If people pay money for something, they'll try to convince themselves that they have made a good purchase, even if they haven't, and in a Tarot reading, they will convince themselves of the validity of the guidance you offer simply because they have paid you. However, it is incumbent upon you not to take advantage of this weakness in human nature and to make sure, to the best of your ability, that your reading is as good as it can possibly be.

Now, I don't overcharge, but I don't undercharge, either. I won't charge exorbitant fees or ridiculous money, which I could easily do, because I refuse to exploit people's vulnerability. But I do provide a service that has to be paid for. After all, even Tarot readers have to eat!

I once read somewhere the following cynical quote, "All the best psychiatrists in America agree that charging the patient a high fee has a strong therapeutic effect." Cynical? Yes, but I think there is a lot of truth in it!

Before I leave the subject of money, I will give you one more reason for charging a reasonable fee: it's very important for the welfare of the client that he or she does not become dependent on you. You do not wish to set yourself up as their personal guru. They can come and see you once a year, that's fine, even every six months.

I feel uncomfortable if a client returns within three months, unless a new, major upset has occurred in their life and it's an emotional emergency. I tend to discourage people coming back too often, and one way I have of discouraging them is to ask a good enough fee that keeps them from seeing me too regularly. After all, they have to take charge of their own lives. This is what I try to help them do, and this is where we come to the next suggestion, and that is: don't give advice.

Suggestion Number Three
Don't Give Advice

I have already mentioned that you should not give legal or medical advice. Actually, you should try not to give advice of any sort. You don't know the full ins and outs of the situation. You don't know all the personalities involved. You probably only get a brief glimpse of the situation and it will be biased from the client's point of view, so what do you do?

They come to see you because they think you know the answers to their problems. After all, you're supposed to be the all-wise, all-knowing psychic. The fact that your own wife is suing you for divorce, the bank manager wants to call in your overdraft, the police have found heroin in your back yard and your son has been arrested for armed robbery is of no concern to your client.

She's paying you to do the impossible, to solve her problems. It doesn't dawn on her that if you knew everything, you'd be living in Monte Carlo in the royal palace! All the psychiatrists, social workers, counsellors, etc., are in exactly the same position. They can't solve their client's problems either. I bet they can't even solve their own problems! All they can really do is to help people to help themselves.

When I first started, it was a baptism of fire. I had hundreds of clients and I didn't know what I was doing. I was really thrown in at the deep end. It's not a way I would recommend anyone to start.

It was accidental in my case, but you see, I put an advertisement in the local paper and I was absolutely inundated, because fortune telling and Tarot card reading are very popular in Ireland, where I first started. I thought I'd get maybe three or four phone calls, but I got hundreds—it was amazing! Anyway, I had to learn fast that I couldn't give advice, simply because in nine cases out of ten, I didn't know the answer; and even if I thought I did, I'd probably give the wrong answer.

A lot of the time, the client will do what they want anyway, no matter what you say. They simply want confirmation.

I figured that giving advice about a situation that I really didn't know that much about might well do more harm than good, so I decided to go a different route. I reasoned that my responsibility is to foretell the outcome according to what I see in the cards, rather than give advice. Of course, clients do expect the Tarot to tell the future to a certain extent.

Of course, this is what I do nowadays, and I try to make sure that I predict positive outcomes rather than negative ones. If you predict this, it usually happens, particularly because of the self-fulfilling prophecy principle previously mentioned.

So, my advice is to avoid giving advice! Having said this, I do give advice occasionally when the solution seems so obvious to me that I would be irresponsible if I did not give my opinion. You have to use common sense rather than stick to rigid rules, I believe.

I do remember, years ago, one talented reader making the point that, if she's temped to give advice, she emphasises that her advice is her own personal opinion and has nothing to do with her psychic abilities. She emphasises that her advice does not necessarily have any more validity than anybody else's. She even goes so far as to put away the cards and make a cup of tea for the client before she discusses the matter. This is to disassociate her personal advice from her psychic reading. It emphasises that her opinions have nothing to do with her psychic ability, but are simply an interaction between one human being and another.

Now, I personally don't go as far as this. One is because I haven't got the time, and two, I can't make tea properly; but I like the philosophy behind the idea. It's food for thought and I advise you to think about it anyway.

Suggestion Number Four:
Don't Predict Gloom and Doom

I have already touched on this, but it won't hurt to mention it again. Unfortunately, I have heard many horror stories from distressed clients who have seen Tarot readers who really believe they see death, destruction and misery, and they feel it's their sacred duty to inform the wretched client of their impending doom.

Some readers are more responsible, and they don't tell the client what disaster they see, but the funny thing is, the client senses something is wrong anyway, and they can leave quite distressed.

I do have a horror story to impart. This took place many years ago and it illustrates the harm done by readers who use the Tarot for evil rather than good. In many cases these readers are not doing the evil intentionally, but because they are hampered by fanatical and mistaken belief in what they are doing. They feel that they must impart to the often-vulnerable client the imagined negativity they see, on the grounds that they must be completely honest. A very dangerous procedure indeed, and this true story will illustrate what I am talking about.

One day, a young man came in to see me in a terrible, terrible state. He had lived a very tragic life. His father had sexually abused him when he was young. On top of this he had drifted unhappily through his life; not sticking to any job, always broke, not forming any relationships. To cap it all, his sister had died of Leukaemia a year before he came in to see me. He was very close to his sister, so he was upset. In the depths of his despair, he decided to consult a notorious Spanish Tarot reader, resident in Dublin, Ireland.

This Spanish crackpot duly informed him that he would end up in a mental hospital. He would go to London and get engaged, but the engagement would be broken off. He would never go with women, but instead turn to men for sexual satisfaction, and basically his life would not exactly be a bed of roses. That night, the young man went home and tried to hang himself. Fortunately, someone saved him and he continued on his unhappy way.

One year later, with the prophecies from Spain still preying on his mind, he decides to come and see the great guru Mark Lewis.

He arrived shaking like a leaf, not surprisingly in view of his past experiences with psychics. His very first question to me was, "You're not a black witch, are you?" It seems that this Spanish fellow claimed that he was. Now, when I assured him that I wasn't (people call me many things, but they'll never call me a black witch), he told me the details of his life history and bad experience with the so called "black witch", whereupon I assured him that the reading he received was abject nonsense and that the witch in question knew as much about the Tarot as I did about the care and breeding of Japanese butterflies.

I tried my very best to help him and lift him from the depths of his despair, and I am pleased to say that I made great progress in this endeavour.

To make a long story short, he came to see me a few times, over four years or so, not making a habit of it, making a little steady progress each time. Finally, he disappeared and I didn't hear from him again for a few years. Then one day, I received a phone call from Germany, of all places, and I thought, "Who do I know from Germany?" He'd gone to work there. He thanked me for all I'd done for him.

The interesting part of the story is that one day I happened to read a newspaper story concerning the "black witch" in question. He had committed suicide. The negativity had rebounded on him, it seems.

To lift someone up from the depths of despair is very gratifying, of course. I am not Mother Teresa by any means, and neither are most of us, but you can still do good. There's no reason on earth you have to predict doom and gloom in a Tarot reading. In fact, it is very dangerous and harmful. The ethical part of the game is fraught with enough difficulties without doing deliberate damage like this. Enough said!

Suggestion Number Five:
A few phrases that will be of great assistance to you

"These are not the Ten Commandments. I don't know everything. If I knew everything, I could win the lotto."

"Nothing is cast in tablets of stone."

"This is like looking through frosted glass. I get glimpses but I don't see everything."

"Psychic ability or intuition is not something you can turn on or off like a tap. Sometimes it comes, and sometimes it doesn't."

"It's like electricity: we don't know why it works, but that doesn't stop us from using it."

All these phrases will stop you looking too omnipotent. You don't want them to think you know everything. It encourages dependency, which you don't want. Actually, I prefer my clients slightly sceptical.

Ethics

I don't want them too believing. I want them to realise that I am human, and that I can make mistakes. I don't know everything.

I have mentioned previously my weather forecast analogy. Here is the phrase I use to explain this to the client.

"This is a bit like the weather forecasting service. A forecaster could say it's going to rain next week and they're usually right, that's their job. But occasionally, they do get it wrong, and so do I. I can show you the trends that are coming up, but it's not 100%."

You see, you must give yourself that leeway. You don't want them thinking you're God. Ethics, you see. My goodness, I wonder if I could get elevated to sainthood? Err, perhaps not, I suppose….

Suggestion Number Six
Tell the client what they want to hear—or perhaps not

You will see all sorts of things in the cards which apply to the clients. Some of them will be negative and you have to use great discretion as to whether you mention this or not. My tendency is to play them down or not even mention them at all unless it is a matter of great importance for the client to know what you see. However, as previously mentioned, you have to be very careful not to provoke the self-fulfilling prophecy aspect of things that I have previously referenced.

However, you will also see positive trends that the client would like to hear. You may, of course, be eager to impart this knowledge to the client. However, that can create an ethical problem. What happens if what the client wants to hear is not good for the client to hear? That does sometimes happen you know. So, after you find out what it is the client wants to hear, you must decide, will it do any harm for me to tell this person what they want to hear?

If there's no harm done, then go ahead and tell them, fine. But if harm is possible, don't forget you have to sleep at night, so keep your mouth shut.

Suggestion Number Seven
Your own mindset

This is quite an important suggestion in a way. The stresses in dealing with people's problems can be quite difficult for the reader.

The reality is that you will not succeed all the time. Some people you just will not be able to help. You must acknowledge your limitations. By doing this you will be more effective as a counsellor, and that's what you are as a Tarot reader: you're a counsellor to some degree or other.

The less guilty you feel about your failures, the more your success rate will go up. My point is that no matter how good you are, no matter how experienced, there will be clients that do get away. They'll still walk out the door unhappy. Just a few of them. If you are really good at your work it may only be a tiny few—but a few nevertheless. By winding yourself up about them too much, you will do damage to yourself and decrease your ability to help those that you are able to help.

The point I am making is that a little help is a lot of help, and as a Tarot reader, there's only a limited amount you can do to help them to help themselves. But that limited amount can still be significant if you plant the seed.

Now I've taken up a massive amount of space on ethics, but it's about time someone mentioned the subject in some depth when writing about the Tarot. You've got a great amount of responsibility for people when you're in this business and I wish there had been some guidance on this subject when I first started. Anyway, I believe I've covered it pretty extensively here.

CHAPTER SIX
Interpretation

At this point, now that you know the meanings of the cards and have an understanding of the ethical issues involved in reading them, I shall attempt to teach you the real meat of the matter: how to do a reading in the first place! I think the best way to do this is to take you through the procedure I personally use to do a reading. Before I start, however, I had better explain that there are two schools of thought in Tarot circles as to how you should start the session.

Some Tarot readers will start the reading by asking, "What do you want to know about?" or "What are your questions?" I would personally prefer a more subtle question such as, "Is there anything you would wish to discuss today?"

One school of thought believes that the less questions you ask of the client the better, at least at the beginning of the reading anyway. The reasoning is that the client may think, "Aren't you supposed to be telling me rather than the other way round?" This school of thought feels that the clients will have more respect for you, not to mention credibility in your work, if at least you seem to know something about their concerns before they are even mentioned. It is, of course, more difficult to do it this way, but the reasoning is that the extra effort in establishing credibility is worth it.

The opposing school of thought believes that this is abject nonsense. It would state that the Tarot reader is not a stage mind reader or carnival act. The reasoning is that you are not being paid to tell people what they already know but what they don't know! Clients have questions and they want you to give them answers rather than waste time in a guessing game. The reasoning is that the client will be eager to discuss their issues with you and will be happy to answer your questions in order to help you answer theirs in return.

I shall leave the decision on which route to follow to you, the reader. In the end you will have to decide which way would be best for you personally. I tend to go with the first option, and I find the less questions I ask, the better, not only at the beginning of the reading, but all the way through, right to the very end. I limit myself to only three questions at the very most in a, say, twenty–thirty-minute reading.

Of course I do have the advantage of reading the person's palm before going on to the Tarot. Of course, palmistry is beyond the scope of this book, but I do find it a very useful skill to use in combination with the Tarot because once I read a client's palm, I know most of what I need to know about him or her, including a very good idea what their questions and concerns are. That means that when I go on to the Tarot, I know all about the person without having to ask them a single question! Their palms have told me the entire story! Or most of it anyway! In any event the very first spread of the Tarot will tend to give me clues as to what the client's issues are anyway.

A psychic fair promoter once told me that the strongest combination for a reader to use is the palm and Tarot combined. I have indeed found that to be true. Of course, I fully realise that my reader is going to have enough trouble learning how to read the Tarot without having to worry about palmistry as well! Besides, this book is supposed to be about reading the cards rather than reading the hands!

The question now arises, if that is the case, then how does our neophyte Tarot reader find out what is the main concern going on in the mind of the client without asking him or her outright? Well, as time goes by and the less neophyte the reader becomes, the easier the whole thing is because intuition begins to take over. The more readings you do the more intuitive you become.

Of course that begs the question, "In the meantime what does the neophyte do to find out what the client's concern is while waiting for the months and years of experience to transpire?"

Well, the partial answer to this is that, if you are observant, a lot of information about the client can be gleaned before they even sit down for a reading. For example, if a client makes an appointment to see you, they might say certain things that are a bit of a giveaway to you. A passing remark such as, "I can't see you on Tuesday because I have a doctor's appointment," or, "I can only see you in the evening because I'm working during the daytime," or even something like, "My husband doesn't believe in this sort of thing," can give you quite a lot of information without you having to ask a single question. You know from the above remarks, as an example, that your client may have a health problem (first remark), or that he or she is working (second remark) or that she is married to a sceptical husband (third remark). This can be noted and used during the reading.

Interpretation

At psychic fairs a potential client will often say something like, "My daughter is in the lecture area," or, "My husband is over there having a reading." So now you know the person had a daughter and a husband! If they sit down and have a reading with you, keep this in mind when you do the reading.

Now, some serious Tarot exponents may regard this as cheating. I don't—I regard it as being streetwise! After all, you didn't search out the information since it came to you unsolicited. You just made use of it after it came to you and I think you are perfectly entitled to do that.

Of course, this is hardly enough, so you will have to be on the lookout for more clues. This may well come from the appearance of your client. That person may look healthy or unhealthy, rich or poor, slovenly or well dressed, stressed out or happy go lucky. This combined with the meanings of the cards will give you more information about the situation.

However, your main source of information will come from the cards themselves, especially the very first spread. There will be clues in the cards in front of you as to what the issue is on the mind of the client. Please bear in mind that most issues come under only a few categories. I have never counted the categories, but I bet there are not more than a dozen or so. We think we are all different, but in reality, we are all the same. Human beings generally all have variations of the same problems. Here are a few of them:

1. Unhappiness in love. This is a major one and will come up very frequently.

2. Health issues. Obviously, something to watch out for if you have an older client, although it can also occur with younger people, too.

3. Career issues. People are often unhappy in their work and want a change.

4. Financial matters. People are always looking for more money and ironically pay you some of it to find out if there is more of it coming their way! Still, I must not be cynical....

You will find that ninety percent of your clients will have issues on their minds that come under one of the four categories above. Each category will have various subcategories, of course, but most questions that are on the mind of the client will be there somewhere.

The same questions will come up again and again, such as:

"Will I lose my job?"

"Will I get a promotion?"

"Does John love me?" (OK. It doesn't have to be "John"!)

"Will my health improve?"

"Will my children do well in life?"

"Will I win the Lotto?" (The answer is usually no!)

After a while a Tarot reader starts to see a pattern emerging over the months and years of the same questions coming up all the time, can spot them coming, and provide answers to them, because he or she gets so used to them.

To go off at a temporary tangent, just writing the above has given me an idea—a frivolous idea but an idea nevertheless. I mentioned in the first chapter that I am a magician as well as a Tarot reader. I happen to know a magic trick with a fortune-telling theme. Nothing to do with the Tarot, but it relates to what I just wrote about the questions that clients come up with. I think I will probably stick it in this book somewhere, probably the last chapter, as a final reward for reading to the end! It is just a fun thing for a party or to be shown to your friends and not to be taken seriously. There! It is amazing what an author can think of on the spur of the moment while writing!

All right. The tangent is over and I suppose I had better get back to business. I do believe a Tarot reader can start to ask a question or two to clarify matters but not straight away at the very beginning. I believe that it should happen a little later in the reading when the confidence of the client is gained, and I will explain shortly how you can do this. For the moment I think the best thing for me to try to explain is how, to some degree, you can figure out what is on the mind of your client and what it really is that they want to find out from you.

Probably the best way for me to proceed is to take you through an imaginary reading step by step and explain what I would say and why I would say it. Of course, a lot depends on what sort of client you have in front of you. This is where things are going to get a little complicated since you could have a male client or a female client. Usually a female, although probably 25% of clients in my experience are male.

Interpretation

But there are other possibilities, too. Your client could be young or old, a student or a businessman, a police officer or a social worker, a civil servant or a factory worker, an employee or an employer and so on and so forth. I even had a nun come for a reading once! No kidding... still, that is another story for another time!

I now have to decide what kind of person is coming for my imaginary reading. Let me think. All right—I have just thunk! I imagine a very common scenario is a lady around 40 or so years of age, reasonably well dressed but looking a bit tired and stressed out. Not a lot to go on, is there? In fact, although I just invented this fictional lady, even I don't know anything else about her!

I am now going to give her a reading just as if she was in my presence. You can all listen in to (OK—read!) what I am about to say to her. I promise that her privacy will not be compromised since she doesn't actually exist in the first place! I am actually going to take a deck of Tarot cards as I type and select ten cards at random on her behalf. Right now, I have no idea what these cards are going to be or what they reveal about this lady. I think this is the best way for you to see how I approach a reading. It will also help me to explain the structure that I use.

I will use the Rider-Waite deck for this. I am actually going to shuffle the cards in a moment. Normally, if the client is right in front of me, I would get that person to do the shuffling, but for obvious reasons of invisibility, I will shuffle the deck myself right now on her behalf.

When you do this with a real live person, you can get a bit of an idea regarding their attitude—plus, what you can pick up from their body language and demeanour—just by the way they shuffle the cards. For example, if they mix the cards face upwards, you can deduce that they are a very open type of person, not secretive in any way. If the cards are shuffled face down, it doesn't mean much, because most people shuffle that way. But if the face-down shuffle is combined with the client holding the cards close to the body, that could well be a sign that they are a little secretive in nature and don't wish to give away much information to you. This possibility is often compounded by negative or guarded body language.

If a client shuffles in a sloppy, untidy manner it could well mean that this person is not fully concentrating on the reading and you will have not have gained his or her attention. Of course, the cynic in me tends to think that all it really means is that they don't play cards much and are not used to them! After all, Tarot cards tend to be much larger than regular playing cards anyway, thus making them more awkward to shuffle.

On the other hand, if they shuffle the cards neatly and thoroughly, that can possibly mean a very thorough person who likes to see a job done perfectly. A bit of a perfectionist, in fact.

I should mention that all the above observations are not cast in tablets of stone. However, they should be kept in mind as you do the reading.

After the cards are shuffled, I normally ask the client to cut the deck into three portions towards me. Let us assume the client is sitting directly opposite me. Some readers prefer the client to sit at right angles to them so they are at the side rather than directly opposite. They feel they gain more rapport that way. By all means go for it if you prefer that option. I did try it myself at one point but found it just wasn't for me.

Anyway, as before I will cut the cards on behalf of this imaginary lady. I now complete the cut and gather all the cards together once more. At this point I spread the cards in one long face-down row on the table and request the client to select any ten cards. As explained in this imaginary example I will now do it on her behalf. I then lay the cards out face upwards in what is known as the Pyramid Spread. Here is a picture showing what the spread looks like:

The Pyramid Spread

Interpretation

I suppose I had better go over the cards shown in the picture in case you can't see them properly. By all means take them out of your own deck and lay them out as shown in the photograph.

The card at the very top of the pyramid is the Knight of Cups. Below that in the second row from the top (left to right) we have the Ten of Wands and the Six of Pentacles. In the third row we have from left to right the Two of Wands, the Nine of Wands, and the Four of Wands. Finally, on the fourth and bottom row we have the High Priestess, the Empress, the Emperor and the Hierophant.

All right. At this point I have no idea what is on this lady's mind. However, I shall just read the cards and show you what I would say to this person if this was a real live scenario. After I do so I will try to analyse what I said and why I said it.

"As I am looking at the cards, I can see that you are not at the high point of your life. You seem to be taking stock of things and re-evaluating the path you are going on. One road goes to the left and one road goes to the right, and you may not be quite sure which path you should follow. I do believe a hand will come as if from out of the sky and guide you on the correct path. Let me give you some advice. Don't make any decision if you are in a bad mood. Or stressed out. Or confused. Only make decisions when you are in a calm frame of mind, but once you make a decision stick to it. Don't chop and change. After all, sometimes it is better to make the wrong decision rather than no decision at all.

"I see from the cards that you may have learned the hard way in the area of love in the past, but the future seems much better than the past has been. There seems to be a much better path emotionally in the future than there may have been in the past. That is indicated by the Knight of Cups. I am able to tell you that you will not be alone. The Emperor card seems to represent your partner in life, either now or in the future. He seems to have a strong personality and will be financially secure.

"With the Empress card here there are signs that you are a strong personality who doesn't give in easily. You always bounce back. Other people in your situation may go under, but not you. You are a survivor. When life hands you a lemon you can make lemonade out of it.

"The High Priestess here shows to me that you have a guardian angel of some sort. Something watching over you. Some Tarot readers believe this card represents God watching over you, but other psychic readers say no, it means someone that has passed away. I usually find it is someone who has passed away. You know, someone can be in the next room, you can't see them, but you know they are there. That person or spirit or whatever form it takes is there and watches over you from time to time.

"The Six of Pentacles shows me that you can be a good spender. You see something you like; you buy it first and worry about the consequences later! That is probably why you are sitting here now, so I had better not complain!

"From the Ten of Wands I see that you work quite hard, possibly even too hard. I think you need a bit of a break—possibly a holiday of some kind. Mind you that might be what this card, the Two of Wands means. It does show a possibility of some travel coming up. Either you are going to travel to see someone you have not seen for a long time or they are coming to see you.

"You are going to be quite busy over the next 12 months—and it is good to keep busy. You know the old saying, "You have to lose yourself in action lest you wither in despair." Having said that as I explained previously, it will also be a good idea not to overdo things and take a break occasionally.

"I see a celebration of some sort coming up in the next twelve months. Maybe someone you know is getting married, maybe someone is having a child---I really don't know what it is but I see you being there as part of the celebration and it does make you feel good to be there.

"I see lots of people giving you advice, saying, 'Why don't you do this, why don't you do that?' and you wish they would shut up and mind their own business! They mean well but their own lives are not perfect. Having said that I do see looking at the Hierophant that there is indeed someone in the cards who will indeed give you good advice. This seems to be a professional person such as a doctor or a lawyer or perhaps an accountant—I am not really sure. What I can tell you is that this person is expert in his or her field and is worth listening to.

"Healthwise, no news is good news. I don't really see any bad health issues surrounding you in the cards, although I always tell people that if they feel sick they should see a doctor, not a Tarot reader!

"There is just one thing though. I think you worry too much according to the Nine of Wands. You can handle the major calamities of

Interpretation

life—it is the small things that seem to get you down. You would be a little bit like the oak tree in the field that can withstand the thunder, the lightning and the storms, but the little insects get to the wood and bring the tree down. You would be a bit like that. Still, the good news is that if we look at that Nine of Wands again, you should know that Wands represent confusion but because it is a Nine it represents the end of confusion. That is because Nine is a number of endings. That means that your confusion and worry are coming to an end.

"Let me give you some advice: take things one day at a time. Don't worry about yesterday—you cannot saw sawdust. Don't worry about tomorrow. All life requires is that you get out of bed in the morning, go about your daily business and then go back to bed at night. In other words, just take one day at a time.

"Here is a little nursery rhyme that might prove useful:

'For every ailment under the Sun
There is a remedy or there is none
If there be one try to find it
If there be none then never mind it'

"The future looks positive for you. Now before I go on to a more powerful spread of cards, do you have any questions? Is there anything you wanted to ask me?"

ANALYSIS

The above is an example of a typical reading I might do for a client who would select those particular cards and fit the description of the imaginary lady in question. Probably the best way for me to analyse it is simply to reproduce it and then put my observations in red type so I can explain why I said what I said at various points. Here we go:

I recommend that when the cards are first laid out you look them over silently for a few moments. This has a twofold purpose. One is that it builds up the suspense and slight tension for the client, and two, it gives you a chance to look at the cards and receive an initial impression regarding the layout, and form a bit of an idea on the best way to proceed.

Some Tarot readers have specific meanings for specific parts of a spread. I don't bother and I just go all over the place and don't worry too much about placement. If I do see one card adjacent to another that seems to link a part of the story, I will use it, but it isn't necessary since there are other cards in the spread that I can probably link together just as easily.

Once I have built up the suspense and have figured out a rough idea of what I might say, I start the reading.

"As I am looking at the cards, I can see that you are not at the high point of your life. You seem to be taking stock of things and re-evaluating the path you are going on. One road goes to the left and one road goes to the right, and you may not be quite sure which path you should follow. I do believe a hand will come as if from out of the sky and guide you on the correct path."

This is a good opening and it lets me get started. Normally I say the above lines when I see specific cards, such as the Justice card (balancing the scales, which can refer to making decisions), the Two of Swords or the Judgement card, but in this case those cards were not in this particular spread. However, I know that the very fact that someone has come to me for a reading may well mean that they have something to decide.

"Let me give you some advice. Don't make any decision if you are in a bad mood. Or stressed out. Or confused. Only make decisions when you are in a calm frame of mind, but once you make a decision stick to it. Don't chop and change. After all, sometimes it is better to make the wrong decision rather than no decision at all."

This is good advice which I think I must have gotten from some self-help book or other. I strongly advise reading self-help books as there is often advice in them that you can pass on to your clients even if you don't necessarily follow the advice yourself!

"I see from the cards that you may have learned the hard way in the area of love in the past, but the future seems much better than the past has been. There seems to be a much better path emotionally in the future than there may have been in the past. That is indicated by the Knight of Cups. I am able to tell you that you will not be alone. The Emperor card seems to represent your partner in life, either now or in the future. He seems to have a strong personality and will be financially secure."

I was disappointed to see in this spread not very much in the way of matters pertaining to love except for this one card, the Knight of Cups. That is because I know that love is often a very important part of the reading and in fact the most frequent area of concern for the client, especially if the client is female. It may well be the reason the person has

Interpretation

come to see me. Because of this I looked for the suit of Cups, but alas the Knight of Cups was the only one I could find.

At this point I would normally look at the client to see the reaction when I mention that she may have learned the hard way in love. This tells me a lot and it may well give the game away as to why she has come to see me. If things are not going well at the moment in love it may well show up in her reaction, whether that reaction is a slight tearing up, or a confirmatory nod of the head or perhaps, as often happens, a vocal outburst of, "You're not kidding!" Although I said "in the past", the reaction may well show that the unhappiness is in the present rather than the past. This is where you have to use your intuition or gut feeling, which is all psychic ability is when you get down to basics.

Incidentally, this may be a good place to mention that in many cases when you do a reading, the client may give you no reaction at all during the course of the entire session. Not a smile, or even the slightest indication of facial expression or body language. He or she will hardly say a word to you and let you do all the talking.

People that know me well may make cynical remarks that this shouldn't be a problem for me since I like the sound of my own voice anyway! However, in reality it does make the reading more difficult if there is no feedback from the client. Even worse is the possibility of the client showing a negative reaction, which is even worse than no reaction at all! This can be disconcerting to a neophyte Tarot reader who may tend to panic a little and think that the reading is not going over very well.

I learned a long time ago never to panic when this happens and to continue to state what I see in the cards regardless of the reaction or lack thereof coming from the client. You just plough on and ignore the person and simply focus on what you see in the cards. You will often be amazed that when the reading is finally over to see how the client will relax and sing your praises, saying how accurate you were, and you will then heave an inward sigh of relief that things weren't as bad as you thought they were!

Mind you, sometimes the opposite happens and you will see a client nodding her head repeatedly at everything you say, but you get a gut feeling that they are just agreeing to be polite. When this happens, I may well pause and ask, "Does this make sense to you?" in order to get at the truth.

One technique I use in a situation where the client is freezing up and showing a lack of reaction as just described, is to use humour in the reading. I don't want belly laughs from the client. After all, I am not performing in a comedy club, and clients have serious issues and often have nothing to laugh about. However, I do try to make a light humorous remark during the reading to at least get a smile and relax the tension.

For example, I might say something like, "I see that you and your partner in life will be financially stable. He will make the money and you will spend it for him!" Or to certain persons that it seems applicable, "You worry too much. You worry about this, you worry about that. If you had nothing to worry about you would worry in case you were overlooking something to worry about!"

This use of humour in a reading, of course, has to suit the personality of the Tarot reader, but if you have the temperament for it you do have a very useful tool at your disposal. You go for smiles rather than laughs, and it make things a lot easier when you have slightly resistant clients.

All right. Back to our imaginary lady client! I interpret the presence of the Knight of Cups and the Emperor card as being one and the same person, and as mentioned in a previous chapter, to me the Emperor represents someone who is financially secure with a strong personality.

"With the Empress card here there are signs that you are a strong personality who doesn't give in easily. You always bounce back. Other people in your situation may go under but not you. You are a survivor. When life hands you a lemon you can make lemonade out of it.

"The High Priestess here shows to me that you have a guardian angel of some sort. Something watching over you. Some Tarot readers believe this card represents God watching over you, but other psychic readers say no, it means someone that has passed away. I usually find it is someone who has passed away. You know, someone can be in the next room, you can't see them but you know they are there. That person or spirit or whatever form it takes is there and watches over you from time to time."

Here I am interpreting in the above two paragraphs the meanings of both the Empress card and the High Priestess as I see them. Of course, as previously explained these meanings are *my* meanings rather than yours, but at least it will give you an idea how I approach a reading.

"The Six of Pentacles shows me that you can be a good spender. You see something you like; you buy it first and worry about the consequences later! That is probably why you are sitting here now so I had better not complain!"

Another example of how I use humour in a reading. It also gives you an idea how I use the picture on the Six of Pentacles to help me interpret the meaning of the card. To me it represents someone giving money away freely, but if I wanted, I could make it mean a person with a charitable nature. The scales in the picture could mean something else to you, but right now I can't think what so I will leave that to you! However, as always the point I am making is that the meaning of a card depends on what *you* want it to mean.

"From the Ten of Wands I see that you work quite hard, possibly even too hard. I think you need a bit of a break—possibly a holiday of some kind. Mind you that might be what this card, the Two of Wands means. It does show a possibility of some travel coming up. Either you are going to travel to see someone you have not seen for a long time or they are coming to see you."

If you study the pictures on both the Ten of Wands and the Two of Wands you will see how I came to make the interpretation I did.

"You are going to be quite busy over the next 12 months—and it is good to keep busy. You know the old saying, 'You have to lose yourself in action lest you wither in despair.' Having said that, as I explained previously it will also be a good idea not to overdo things and take a break occasionally.

Again I am saying this because of the presence of the Ten of Wands.

"I see a celebration of some sort coming up in the next twelve months. Maybe someone you know is getting married, maybe someone is having a child—I really don't know what it is, but I see you being there as part of the celebration and it does make you feel good to be there."

Although I don't mention the card here, I am picking up the "celebration" because of the Four of Wands since the image there seems to indicate celebration as it pertains to my personal meaning of the card.

"I see lots of people giving you advice, saying 'Why don't you do this, why don't you do that?' and you wish they would shut up and mind their own business! Again note the use of humour here. "They mean well but their own lives are not perfect. Having said that I do see looking at the Hierophant that there is indeed someone in the cards who will indeed give you good advice. This seems to be a professional person such as a doctor or a lawyer or perhaps an accountant—I am not really sure. What I can tell you is that this person is expert in his or her field and is worth listening to."

Something very interesting just happened here. I didn't even notice it until a moment ago. In the above segment I actually made a mistake! For some odd reason I confused the meaning of the Hierophant with that of the Magician card! Possibly because of the slight similarity in the image because in both pictures the two characters are wearing the colour red and that confused me somewhat.

The other reason for the mistake is that I am writing this late at night and I am a little tired. However, this brings up a very profound point. Actually, two profound points, but let me get this one out of the way first. It is a very strange thing I have noticed over many years of doing readings. The more tired I am, the more accurate the readings!

For example, when I do psychic fairs, I can get pretty exhausted as the day progresses, but the more exhausted I get the more accurate the readings seem to be.

This baffled me quite a bit until I analysed it and figured out why. I think what happens is that the conscious analytical part of the mind tends to shut down and the unconscious psychic part takes over to some extent. Since the conscious thinking part of my mind is too tired to think any more the burden is transferred to the subconscious mysterious part of the mind, which tunes in somehow to the real power of the Tarot without any effort.

The second point is that it doesn't really make any difference what card shows up. As I have previously stated, the cards are no more than a random stimulator to the imagination, creativity and intuition of the reader. It is the interpretation of the cards rather than the cards themselves that is the important thing. Therefore, it doesn't make the slightest difference to the client what meaning the Tarot reader ascribes to the card as long as it fits her situation.

"Healthwise, no news is good news, I don't really see any bad health issues surrounding you in the cards, although I always tell people that if they feel sick they should see a doctor not a Tarot reader!"

It is important in this first spread of cards that you cover all the main areas of the client's life at least in a general sense. That is, love, work, money and in this case health. This is because by doing so you

Interpretation

can gauge the reaction of the Querent when you mention each area. If you pick up a little hint of a reaction or even a micro-expression when you cover a certain specific category, you do get a clue as to what is on their mind without having to ask them directly.

We have covered all the bases in the above reading except health. Since I don't see any indication from any of the cards concerning health, I do have to say something else with regard to this so I can judge the reaction of the client. I have already explained in Chapter Five the lines I used in the above segment referring to "no news is good news" to cover health matters.

Now, the point I am trying to make is that if there is some issue with any of the categories such as love, work, health or money, the client may well show a reaction which will make you tend to focus in on that area. Let us take health for example; if you have misjudged the situation and the Querent shows little or even strong signs of disagreement, you at least know which path you should follow during the rest of the reading. That is why the first spread is so important. It gives you the information so that when you do subsequent spreads you are in a stronger position to proceed.

"There is just one thing though. I think you worry too much according to the Nine of Wands. You can handle the major calamities of life—it is the small things that seem to get you down. You would be a little bit like the oak tree in the field that can withstand the thunder, the lightning and the storms, but the little insects get to the wood and bring the tree down. You would be a bit like that. Still, the good news is that if we look at that Nine of Wands again you should know that Wands represent confusion, but because it is a Nine it represents the end of confusion. That is because Nine is a number of endings. That means that your confusion and worry are coming to an end."

"Let me give you some advice: take things one day at a time. Don't worry about yesterday—you cannot saw sawdust. Don't worry about tomorrow. All life requires is that you get out of bed in the morning, go about your daily business and then to back to bed at night. In other words just take one day at a time.

"Here is a little nursery rhyme that might prove useful:

'For every ailment under the Sun
There is a remedy or there is none

*If there be one try to find it
If there be none then never mind it'"*

This last sequence is based on the wonderful book by Dale Carnegie, *How To Stop Worrying and Start Living*. I have already mentioned the importance of studying self-help books so you can impart the information therein to the client. Well this book on worry is the one I quote from most frequently. I can strongly recommend studying it not only so that you can impart advice from it to your client, but also to help you control worry in your own life.

The reason I have used the advice in this imaginary reading is that you will recall that my initial description of this mythical lady client was that she looked a little stressed out.

"The future looks positive for you. Now before I go on to a more powerful spread of cards, do you have any questions? Is there anything you wanted to ask me?"

These are *very* important questions to ask the Querent at the end of the reading. Quite frankly, when I ask these questions myself, approximately 90% of the time the client simply says "No. That is fine so far," and in some cases says, "No. That was really accurate." However, this is because, as I stated earlier, I usually read the palm before I read the Tarot and most of the information I need is on the palms of the client. In your case, this will not be the situation, since unlike myself you are not a palmist (unless you are of course!). However, you won't need to be since at this point the client will usually pepper you with questions, and of course this will help you with subsequent spreads as the reading continues. You will hear them say such things as, "Is there nothing about this or that?" (whatever this or that might be) or perhaps, "You haven't told me anything about..." (whatever they want to know). They will also ask you about certain things you said in the reading and of course you can respond to all these questions, and most importantly, they will give you more information to focus on during the rest of the session.

There will, of course, also be times when they say that they have no questions and you can probably deduce from that they are satisfied with the reading you have given them so far.

At this point you gather up the tabled cards to get ready for the second and more powerful spread. However, we will get to that a bit later

Interpretation

on. Right now, I am going to give you another sample reading where, although it will use exactly the same cards as the reading I just described, the scenario regarding the client will be completely different. I am doing this to demonstrate to you that, as I have stated previously, the same cards can mean different things to different people. The cards don't change but the people do.

This scenario will be a well-dressed and articulate middle-aged man with an air of authority. He could well be a businessman or at least have a highly paid job since he is very expensively dressed, wearing tasteful jewellery and an expensive looking watch. Now you don't necessarily have to remember or even take much notice of these details because the person is sitting right in front of you and your intuition and, yes—psychic ability will take it all in anyway at a subconscious level.

Here we go:

"The Emperor card shows that you have a strong personality. You are very independent, and you don't like to be ordered about or told what to do by other people. You like to make your own mind up about things and go your own way. In fact, if someone tells you what to do, even if you know they are right, you would do the opposite!

"The Ten of Wands shows that you are not afraid of hard work. In fact, you need to keep busy, otherwise you would get bored very quickly. I do see you being very financially stable in the future. However, the Six of Coins shows that any money that comes to you seems to be through your own efforts rather than anything that is just given to you on a silver platter. There are no long-lost uncles in South America!

"With both the Emperor and the Empress card here this shows a good strong ongoing relationship that will build, grow and develop; you will not be alone in your old age anyway!

"The High Priestess is a marriage card. Are you a married gentleman? You are? Yes—I thought so because of the Emperor and the Empress card coming together in the same spread along with both the Hierophant and the High Priestess in the same row, since these tend to be marriage cards. Out of curiosity, have you been married twice? No? The reason I say this is that with the Nine of Wands here there are some signs that you may have learned the hard way in the past in the area of love. I think there may well have been an old relationship in the past which was important at the time but has since faded away.

"You are full of life and have an adventurous nature and are always willing to try new things.

"I do see that you have travelled extensively in the past and in fact looking at these cards I think I see a possibility of a trip around you in the next twelve months. Possibly business related although I am not quite sure.

"I do see a celebration coming up within the next twelve months. It may well be business related. However, it can also be a sign that someone you know is getting married, especially with these marriage cards showing up in this bottom row.

"The future is quite positive for you and in this spread there seems to be more good than bad. Now before I lay out a more powerful spread which should give me more information, is there anything you wish to ask or discuss with me?"

ANALYSIS

"The Emperor card shows that you have a strong personality. You are very independent, and you don't like to be ordered about or told what to do by other people. You like to make your own mind up about things and go your own way. In fact, if someone tells you what to do, even if you know they are right you would do the opposite!"

The reasoning for the above statements is twofold. The man in question gives off that impression by his demeanour and appearance. This is amplified by the presence of the Emperor card, of which generally speaking the meaning fits the above commentary.

"The Ten of Wands shows that you are not afraid of hard work. In fact, you need to keep busy, otherwise you would get bored very quickly. I do see you being very financially stable in the future. However, the Six of Coins shows that any money that comes to you seems to be through your own efforts rather than anything that is just given to you on a silver platter. There are no long-lost uncles in South America!"

Note the use of humour in the last sentence. When I say that it often raises a smile! I have referred previously to how the use of a little light humour can improve the atmosphere and this is another example of it.

The image on the Ten of Wands in the second row from the top does give the impression of hard work. That coupled with the impression that this person might well be a businessman does tend to give the impression of a very busy person who works quite hard.

The Six of Pentacles/Coins which is adjacent to the Ten of Wands triggers off images of money being spent, which in turn combined with the prosperous appearance of the client results in the interpretation of financial stability which is applied to the gentleman in question.

"With both the Emperor and the Empress card here, this shows a good, strong, ongoing relationship that will build, grow, and develop; you will not be alone in your old age anyway!"

In the lowest row of the pyramid it can be seen that the Emperor and Empress are adjacent to each other, which does seem to give a vibe of a relationship and seems to be the obvious interpretation. Of course, you do not really know if this man is married (let us assume he is not wearing a wedding ring), divorced, single and unattached or even, for all I know, a widower, so I do have to tread carefully here. That is why I do not state outright that the Emperor and Empress cards represent an ongoing relationship at the time of the reading. However, it could well mean a relationship that is going to transpire in the future. You do have to leave this mildly ambiguous for the moment. However, in the following segment you do something to clarify things a lot better.

"The High Priestess is a marriage card. Are you a married gentleman? You are? Yes—I thought so because of the Emperor and the Empress card coming together in the same spread along with both the Hierophant and the High Priestess in the same row since these tend to be marriage cards. Out of curiosity, have you been married twice? No? The reason I say this is that with the Nine of Wands here there are some signs that you may have learned the hard way in the past in the area of love. I think there may well have been an old relationship in the past which was important at the time but has since faded away."

This is a tricky part of the reading and you do have to be streetwise to handle it. In other words, you have to find out the relationship status of the client. I have already mentioned the wisdom of keeping direct questions to a minimum, especially at the beginning of a reading, since it is essential you gain the confidence of the client. However, this is one of the occasions that you really have to do it in order to clarify matters.

You therefore enquire in an offhand casual manner as if in a mere afterthought, "Are you a married gentleman?" If the answer is, "Yes," then you have a better idea which path the reading should go. In practice you will often find that the client will nod affirmatively when you mention "a strong relationship that will build and grow," so you kind of know in advance of the question what the response will be. Your intuition will tell you. However, you can't always rely on intuition, so the question is still necessary.

In the above example the client says "Yes," but you need to fish a bit more. It is an unfortunate statistic that people over forty have often been married twice. I got that information from an astrologer once! Since my imaginary client is middle aged, the odds are quite strong that he has indeed been married twice.

If you get it right, he will be most impressed. If you get it wrong, as I did in the fictional example above, I can sneakily get out of trouble by explaining that there are signs that he may have learned the hard way in the past in the area of love and the old relationship has now faded away! Sneaky, I know!

However, it illustrates again the wisdom of the streetwise approach! Mind you, it is not really cheating because the the Nine of Wands does indeed show that particular meaning! After all, the chap in the picture does indeed look a bit heartily sick at some relationship or other that looks as if it went askew! Well, that is my story anyway and after all, I am the one writing this book, so you will just have to put up with it!

"You are full of life and have an adventurous nature and are always willing to try new things."

This statement is triggered by the Knight of Cups at the very top of the pyramid since it seems to look to me as if the man on the horse is going off to do things he loves (remember Cups represents love) and I just get a feeling of an adventurous nature by simply looking at him. This is compounded by the appearance and articulate demeanour of the client, which seems to confirm the statement.

"I do see that you have travelled extensively in the past and in fact looking at these cards I think I see a possibility of a trip around you in the next twelve months. Possibly business related, although I am not quite sure."

Although I don't mention the specific card here, I base the above statement on the Two of Wands, which to me represents travel because of the image on the card of a man gazing out to sea with a globe of the

Interpretation

world in his hand. I mention possibly business related because my intuition tells me that this man probably does take business trips and travels extensively.

"I do see a celebration coming up within the next twelve months. It may well be business related. However, it can also be a sign that someone you know is getting married, especially with these marriage cards showing up in this bottom row."

The celebration prediction is provoked by the image on the Four of Wands, which does seem to show a couple of people celebrating. And there are indeed suggestions of marriage from the cards in the bottom row of the pyramid.

"The future is quite positive for you and in this spread there seems to be more good than bad. Now before I lay out a more powerful spread which should give me more information, is there anything you wish to ask or discuss with me?"

Again, just as in the previous spread, the above question gives your client a chance to ask for further clarification or bring up things which you may not yet have covered in the reading. This will often result in valuable information which you can expand on in the next spread you lay out.

I am going to give you one more example of a fictional reading, but before I do so I think this is a good point to give you an excellent technique that I, in my great and wondrous wisdom, discovered for the use of a Tarot reader. Some cynical people will say that it is a weird technique and somewhat contradictory to the streetwise approach I am advocating. All I can say in response is that this is a weird business anyway and one more bit of weirdness won't make a lot of difference either way!

The technique is prayer! I told you this was going to be weird! And to make it even weirder, I don't believe in God! But I pray anyway. God knows why. And you can take that last sentence any way you wish.

I now feel inclined to attempt to explain what I am getting at. I shall have to take a deep breath in order to do so. It is a trifle complicated. Again, I regard this as a technique rather than as a religious matter, which it certainly isn't. It will seem a little contradictory, but so be it. I am referring only to psychic readings, although it may or may not have applications elsewhere. One thing is for sure: you won't see this mentioned in too many books on the Tarot, as far as I know, and yet it is a very powerful technique that will improve your readings immensely.

The key is compassion; compassion for your clients. They are often in a vulnerable state when they come to see you. And it is imperative that you approach them in a compassionate and sensitive frame of mind. Prayer is an ideal way to do this. It must be virtually impossible to pray for the client and then at the same time see them as or simply someone who is just there to give you money.

I do it a few moments before they come in to see me and when they remove the selected cards for the spread of the Tarot. With regard to the latter, I say nothing and it creates an atmosphere of silence for a very short time, and this helps develop a spiritual rapport between you and the client. And yet the client has no idea that you have been praying for them and in fact they never find out.

Now, you may get confused when I say you don't have to believe in God to do this, and I find it difficult to explain what I am getting at in this regard.

Let me say that it is a kind of method acting. There is no denying that prayer is an immensely *practical* thing. There is no denying that the very act of prayer is beneficial to the person who is doing the praying. That is because prayer fulfils some very basic psychological needs which everyone shares, whether they are devout believers or downright sceptics. For one thing it gives you a sense of not being alone and sharing your burdens, it relieves stress (and doing a reading can be very stressful at times), and it helps you to put into words what is troubling you and brings clarity to your problems.

From a psychic reading point of view, it creates a spiritual atmosphere and helps you to approach your client with compassion. And when you pray for the client you are also praying for yourself because as I stated in parentheses above, reading for people who have great problems can be stressful for the counsellor whether that counsellor be a social worker, clergyman or even a psychic. Sometimes just the act of prayer can help a reader to be more effective if he doesn't know what to say.

Often if I have no idea how to offer a helpful suggestion or know what to say in a certain situation, I say a silent prayer and just leave it to the cards, God, and the universe to sort it out. And those sources invariably do the job for me.

The act of silent prayer helps to calm ME down and relieve the stress of the reading and the client's burden from MY shoulders. Thus,

Interpretation

it helps me to do a better job. This approach is far more effective than worrying about their body language or asking leading questions to elicit information as some Tarot readers do. God gives you the information.

But you ask, how can you do this if you don't believe in God, as I certainly don't? Well, if I want the undoubted benefit of the above, I have to figure out a way of getting it even though I am not entitled to it. That is the hustler part of me coming out. If you do believe in God you are one step ahead in this, but alas, belief in God tends to bring all sorts of religious trappings and gobbledegook, which you don't want anywhere near a reading.

So how do I get the benefit without the belief? I feel greatly irritated that the believers get the benefit while cynics like me get nothing. Zilch. So what do I do? Well, like any good hustler I STEAL the benefit! And how do I steal it? Well, as I hinted earlier it is a kind of method acting. This is getting a trifle deep so I shall pause, say a prayer (a fraudulent one of a non-believer), take a deep breath and here we go in an attempt to explain my contradictory stance.

It is a well-known psychological trick that feelings often follow action. For example, if you feel miserable, the way to get out of this misery is to ACT happy. And if you act happy by forcing yourself to smile, sing or whistle, an odd thing happens—you suddenly start to feel happy! If you are afraid then the act of acting brave will actually tend to give you courage. If you lack enthusiasm the act of acting enthusiastic will tend to make you enthusiastic. That is because the feeling often follows the action.

So, if you want to believe in God simply for the purpose of the reading, then act as if you believe in him and you will derive the benefit of believing, and you will tend to believe in this power for a short time at least. And the reading will take on more power. When the reading finishes, the client leaves and the illusion is over.

But is it an illusion? Belief in God does bring a certain peace and calm and fortitude, and we can all agree on that, whether we believe in God or not. Dr. Alexis Carrell once said, "Prayer is the most powerful form of energy one can generate. It is a force as real as terrestrial gravity. As a physician, I have seen men, after all other therapy had failed, lifted out of disease and melancholy by the serene effort of prayer.... Prayer, like radium, is a source of luminous, self-generating energy.... In prayer, human beings seek to augment their finite energy by addressing themselves to the infinite source of all energy. When we pray, we link ourselves with the inexhaustible motive power that spins the universe."

Well, I don't really believe in God, but I can believe in "the inexhaustible motive power that spins the universe". So I use that in a psychic reading. Immanuel Kant said, "Why not accept a belief in God because we need such a belief?" Well, I certainly need such a belief when I do psychic readings so for that brief time I convince myself there is a God until the reading is over.

I do realise that all the above guff may not seem very streetwise—but it is, you know. It really is....

All right. Back to the previously scheduled program! Here is one more sample reading and analysis thereof. In the previous examples I used exactly the same spread for two different people. I did this to show you that it isn't the cards so much but how you use them that is important. I wanted to illustrate that you can use exactly the same cards for different people.

Just for a change this last example will take a different direction. I am going to use the Prediction deck, which has no images to guide you in remembering and affixing meanings to the Minor Arcana. In actual fact the Prediction deck is difficult to obtain nowadays since it is out of production. However, there are indeed other decks available with no images on the Minor Arcana, such as the Thoth Tarot or the Tarot of Marseilles.

However, as explained in Chapter Three, there should be no trouble remembering the meanings of the Minor Arcana even without the images by using the memory tricks described in that chapter.

What I propose to do now is to come up with another imaginary client and lay out a random pyramid using the Prediction deck, which will have different meanings for the Minor Arcana than there are on the Rider-Waite deck, although the Major Arcana meanings will remain the same.

Now let me figure out another fictional client. I think this time we will have a younger girl in her early twenties. She's attractive, with a good sense of humour and has never had a reading before.

Interpretation

This does bring up a bit of an ethical issue which I shall try to address. If a young person has never had a Tarot reading before I find that I am in a bit of a catch-22 situation. If I give her a mediocre reading the disadvantage of such is perfectly obvious and I don't think I have to explain it! However, if I give her an excellent reading, that can create a problem, too, albeit a less obvious one.

Let me explain. If someone has never had a reading before and I do a really good job of it, that person may be so enthusiastic about the Tarot that she may get so hooked by it that she might then be making a habit of seeing one psychic after another. In other words, she becomes a psychic addict, and that is *not* a good thing! Some Tarot readers are mediocre, and even worse than that, unethical scam artists of the type I described in Chapter Five.

I do worry somewhat that the excellence of my reading may encourage the client to go on a wrong future path which I may well have started her on in the first place.

I have often been quite surprised at psychic fairs to see that some attendees at these events will not just have one reading from one practitioner but perhaps four or even five! I consider that unhealthy and moreover very expensive!

As I explained in Chapter Five, I tend to discourage clients slightly from coming back to me too often. I believe people have to take charge of their own lives and not depend on psychics like myself who can hardly run their own lives let alone someone else's! The trouble is that if I discourage them too much they may well go and see a less scrupulous Tarot reader, or perhaps a rather more mediocre one, which is nearly as bad.

I do get around this situation by, at the beginning of the session, if the client has never had a reading before, warning them not to become a psychic addict in the future, not to take the reading too seriously and to remember that Tarot card readers don't know everything.

Perhaps I am too fastidious in this policy of mine, but it does help me to sleep at night.

All right. Now that my little sermon is over, I shall shuffle the Prediction Deck and select ten cards for the pyramid spread just as I did before.

Here is what I came up with:

"OK. There are a number of things I see for you in this spread. First of all, I see an opportunity coming up for you in the work area. I don't know if you will go for it. After all, there is an old saying, 'all that glitters is not gold'. Still, having said that, there is another saying, 'nothing ventured, nothing gained', so I will have to let you make up your own mind regarding this.

"I do know that you will succeed in life because of the Chariot card. This is a good card, but it is a tough card, too. That is because it means victory after a struggle. You see the two horses in the picture. We have a black horse and a white horse. The black horse is going one way, the white horse is going another way and the warrior is trying to get the two horses under control. It is a bit of a struggle, but he *does* get them under control. In the same way that you will always get your life under control. Sometimes it will be a bit of a struggle on occasion, but there will always be victory after the struggle.

"The Two of Cups is an excellent card where love is concerned. It does show a good strong loving relationship that will build, grow and develop. Is there someone in your life at the moment? No? Well there will be. It is like waiting for a bus. There will be another one along in a minute!

"I do see some signs that you have learned the hard way in the past where love is concerned. I base this on the Devil card and the Two of Swords, which show stress and conflict in a past relationship. Still, that is in the past. You can read a very interesting book and get to a very interesting page, but you can't keep reading the same page all the time. Sooner or later you have to turn the page and go forward. And I see you doing that and putting the past behind you.

"Ultimately, with the Two of Cups here and the Hierophant, there are very strong signs that you will not be alone in the area of love and it will work out very well, especially with the Hierophant card, which often represents marriage. I am getting a vibe that you have no trouble attracting admirers. The problem is finding the right admirer!

"The Three of Wands indicates that you are at a crossroads in life, thinking, 'Which way am I headed, which way am I going?' One road goes to the left and one road goes to the right and you may not be sure which path to follow. But a hand comes out of the sky right here and shows you the correct path.

"With the Moon card, I see that you can get a little confused and worried on occasion. The good news is that, with the Ten of Wands here, any worries or confusion that are around you at the moment are coming to an end, because ten is a number of endings. Wands is confusion, so with the Ten here, that means an end to confusion.

"Try not to worry about silly things. Remember, a person is hurt not so much by what happens as by their opinion of what happens. And your opinion of what happens is up to you! There is a little rhyme that goes like this:

"Two men looked out from prison bars
One saw mud and the other saw stars.

"In other words, it is not the situation that matters so much as how you perceive that situation.

"Healthwise, no news is good news. I see no major health problems you have to worry about at the present time, although I always tell people that if they feel sick, they should see a doctor, not a Tarot reader.

"Overall, the future looks pretty good. This year will be better than last year and next year will be better than this year.

"Now, I am going to do a more powerful spread, but before I do that, do you have any questions you would like to ask? Does this make sense to you?"

ANALYSIS

"OK. There are a number of things I see for you in this spread. First of all, I see an opportunity coming up for you in the work area. I don't know if you will go for it. After all, there is an old saying, 'all that glitters is not gold'. Still, having said that, there is another saying, 'nothing ventured, nothing gained", so I will have to let you make up your own mind regarding this."

I base this interpretation on seeing in the spread the Page of Swords and the Ace of Wands, which often represent new opportunities to me.

"I do know that you will succeed in life because of the Chariot card. This is a good card, but it is a tough card too. That is because it means victory after a struggle. You see the two horses in the picture. We have a black horse and a white horse. The black horse is going one way, the white horse is going another way and the warrior is trying to get the two horses under control. It is a bit of a struggle, but he *does* get them under control. In the same way that you will always get your life under control. Sometimes it will be a bit of a struggle on occasion, but there will always be victory after the struggle."

This should be self-explanatory and is an expanded version of the example I gave in Chapter Two when discussing the meaning of the Chariot card.

"The Two of Cups is an excellent card where love is concerned. It does show a good strong loving relationship that will build, grow and develop. Is there someone in your life at the moment?"

Again, pretty self-explanatory. However, you will notice I asked a similar question about love as I did in the previous sample reading. The only difference was that I asked the imaginary gentleman if he was a married man. You do almost the same thing here for the same reason. You need to find out her relationship situation in order to tilt the rest of the reading in that direction. You ask the question in the same casual offhand manner. In this fictional scenario she said, "No,"

Interpretation

and you can read how it was handled. If, however, she had said, "Yes," at least you would know which track to follow.

"No? Well there will be. It is like waiting for a bus. There will be another one along in a minute!"

Again, note the use of humour.

"I do see some signs that you have learned the hard way in the past where love is concerned. I base this on the Devil card and the Two of Swords, which shows stress and conflict in a past relationship."

Again, this is based on the actual meaning of the cards.

"Still, that is in the past. You can read a very interesting book and get to a very interesting page, but you can't keep reading the same page all the time. Sooner or later you have to turn the page and go forward. And I see you doing that and putting the past behind you."

More advice of the sort found in self-help books. Again I strongly recommend you read up on this kind of literature as the advice therein can be very useful to present to your clients.

"Ultimately, with the Two of Cups here and the Hierophant, there are very strong signs that you will not be alone in the area of love and it will work out very well, especially with the Hierophant card, which often represents marriage. I am getting a vibe that you have no trouble attracting admirers. The problem is finding the right admirer!"

Because this girl is attractive, it is common sense rather than psychic ability that she would have no trouble finding admirers. Since there is nobody in her life, it is also common sense that she has had trouble finding the right partner!

"The Three of Wands indicates that you are at a crossroads in life, thinking, 'Which way am I headed, where am I going?' One road goes to the left and one road goes to the right and you may not be sure which path to follow. But a hand comes out of the sky right here and shows you the correct path."

The Three of Wands does indeed mean this, or at least it does to me. You simply point out to the client how one wand goes one way and another wand goes another way. However you also point to the centre wand and interpret that as "The hand that comes out of the sky".

"With the Moon card, I see that you can get a little confused and worried on occasion. The good news is that, with the Ten of Wands here, any worries or confusion that are around you at the moment are coming to an end, because ten is a number of endings. Wands is confusion, so with the Ten here, that means an end to confusion."

In the Prediction deck, the Moon card does indeed look a bit on the miserable side! This melancholy meaning does not show up in the Rider-Waite deck, so I only use this worried and miserable interpretation when I use the Prediction deck. The Ten of Wands is self-explanatory, so it doesn't need any clarification from me.

"Try not to worry about silly things. Remember, a person is hurt not so much by what happens as by their opinion of what happens. And your opinion of what happens is up to you! There is a little rhyme that goes like this:

'Two men looked out from prison bars
One saw mud and the other saw stars.

"In other words, it is not the situation that matters so much as how you perceive that situation."

More advice for the client on how to avoid worry. Again the sort of thing you get from self-help books.

"Healthwise, no news is good news. I see no major health problems you have to worry about at the present time, although I always tell people that if they feel sick, they should see a doctor, not a Tarot reader."

Because she looks so young and healthy it is obvious why I make this remark. However, it is always wise to instruct clients to see a doctor if they feel sick.

"Overall, the future looks pretty good. This year will be better than last year and next year will be better than this year."

It is always a good thing to give encouragement to the client before going on to another spread.

"Now, I am going to do a more powerful spread, but before I do that, do you have any questions you would like to ask? Does this make sense to you?"

I have already explained the reasoning for this. Don't neglect it, as by giving the client a chance to ask you questions, you will usually elicit more information you can use as the reading progresses.

Interpretation

The Celtic Cross

I do three spreads in a Tarot reading. Those are the Pyramid Spread, the Celtic Cross, and the Horoscope Spread. I have already explained the Pyramid Spread, so now we will proceed to the Celtic Cross, which is actually a very powerful and popular spread that I imagine is pretty much used by most Tarot readers. The best part about it is that it gives you a chance to elicit some very valuable information from the client without directly asking for it.

When I first started to learn the Tarot, I decided that a good thing for me to do was to visit some readers and have a few readings myself to see what I could learn from the different styles. So I took a pile of money and did just that. If you are rich enough to try this, I would recommend it. I wasn't that rich, but I did it anyway!

Some of the readers were awful and some of them were quite good at their work. However, I did go to one lady in Dublin who was doing readings in a hotel and she did something which I have used ever since. It was very valuable indeed to me and well worth the 15 pounds I gave her for the reading. I am going to pass this on to you now as a reward for reading the book up to this point!

She did the reading with regular playing cards rather than with the Tarot, but I simply modified the procedure to be done with the Tarot and it worked out very well.

It all revolves around what is known as a "Significator card", which means a card that represents the Querent. If the client is female, I use one of the Queens to represent her. For a young man I use a Knight, and for an older man I use a King. But here we come to the clever part! If what I am about to impart is done correctly, it can give you very valuable information on which to base the remainder of your reading. This, combined with the information you have already gleaned from the Pyramid Spread, will help you to focus on the area of most concern to the client.

The best way to explain this is for me give you the sort of thing I might say when I introduce the Significator card. Let us assume the client is a woman, which means in this case I have to use one of the Queens. First, I gather up the Pyramid Spread as it is no longer in use. Before I do so, I look to see if there are any Queens in the spread and if there are, I lay them aside for the moment. I then replace the cards from the spread into the rest of the deck and then go through them all to remove any Queens that are left in there until all four Queens are put aside on the table face upwards.

While doing this, I chatter away, something like this: "OK. Now I need what is known as a Significator card. In other words, a card to represent you. We'll use the four Queens for this. In a moment I am going to ask you to pick out one of the Queens to represent you."

You talk in this vein until you find all four Queens, which you lay face upwards on the table. You now point to each of the Queens in turn and explain the meanings thus: "The Queen of Wands represents health, the Queen of Swords represents work, the Queen of Cups represents love and the Queen of Coins represents money. I would like you to pick the area that would most concern you at the present time. Health, work, love or money? Of course, you are probably interested in all areas, but I just need one to represent you. In any event all areas of your life will come up anyway. I just need one to act as a Significator card."

Now, do you see how clever this is? By this means you find out which is their main area of concern! Once in a while, you may get someone who seems to be torn between two areas, so what I do then is to take the two cards in question, turn them face down, mix them so the client does not know which is which and ask for just one to be selected. I then explain that the other area will come up anyway. I just need one card to represent her.

Once the Querent has selected the Significator card, I lay it face upwards on the table, and then shuffle the other three Queens back into the deck. I then ask the client to shuffle and cut the deck into three packets just as already described in relation to the Pyramid Spread, after which she selects ten cards from the deck spread face down on the table as already explained.

I now take the cards selected and lay out the Celtic Cross, which looks like this:

Interpretation

At this point, when I lay the cards out, I usually mutter a little ritual which doesn't actually mean anything but it adds a little mystical showmanship to the reading. As each card is laid out in turn, I say, "This is the card that crosses you, this is the one that covers you, this is the card that crowns you, this is beneath you, this is behind you, this is in front of you, yourself, your home, your hopes and fears, the final outcome."

The Significator card is concealed to some extent here because of the way the Judgement and the World card are laid on top of it in such a manner so as to obscure it. However, this spread will at least show you how the cards are laid around it and, in the case of the two cards mentioned, on top of it.

Now, traditionally, the normal way that Tarot readers are supposed to interpret the Celtic Cross is to assign certain situations according to the location of each card. For example, the Seven of Wands in the picture, which is second from the top of the vertical row, is supposedly in the "Hopes and Fears" position in traditional Celtic Cross position lore. In theory, I am supposed to interpret the card in relation to the client's hopes and fears, but I find that restricts my flexibility and I simply don't bother with it. Besides, it goes against my streetwise philosophy!

You will also notice that the card below it is the Ace of Swords in the reverse card position, and of course I am supposed to alter the meaning because the card is the wrong way around, as I have previously explained. And of course, as I have also already explained, I don't bother with that either. It just isn't streetwise and after all, I am after results and the client doesn't really care how I get there. I do hope some awful Tarot God in the sky doesn't strike me down with lightning for indulging in such wickedness! All I can say is that this philosophy and procedure work. And work well!

Anyway, you do the reading just as you did before with the Pyramid Spread, but it should be even more powerful than before because, by the tactics I have outlined, you have a lot more information to go on.

The Horoscope Spread

My final spread predicts the next twelve months for the client. This time, twelve cards are selected rather than ten, since there are twelve months in the year. I lay the cards round in a clock-shaped arrangement as shown here:

Each of the twelve positions represents a specific month of the year. January is in the one o'clock position, February in the two o'clock position and so on, right up to December in the twelve o'clock position. The idea of this spread is that you do a rough forecast of the client's life over the next 12 months.

Interpretation

It has to be a "rough" forecast because it is very difficult to be too specific and at the same time also be accurate. This is why I explain at the very beginning of a reading that, as I have mentioned previously, a Tarot session is a bit like a weather forecast and of course even weather forecasters get things wrong sometimes.

You do have the advantage that by now you know quite a bit about the client because of the previous two spreads and the techniques I have already described. This makes it easier to predict future trends and fit them into the meanings of the cards in question.

This is what I say as a bit of a disclaimer before I read the horoscope spread. "This is what we call the Horoscope Spread which, is a basic forecast of the next twelve months. Now sometimes I get the months wrong. I will say things are going to happen in April but in fact they actually happen in May. However, the sequence of events is generally accurate."

I then start the session by first concentrating on the very month the reading is taking place in. Then I have to figure out whereabouts in the month we are at the time of the reading. If the session takes place at the beginning of the month I will figure out where in the spread that particular month is. For example, if I am doing the reading in early September, I start my reading at the card in the nine o'clock position, which of course represents September. However, if the reading is taking place in late September, I will probably start with the card at the ten o'clock position, which of course represents October. If, however, the reading is taking place in the middle of September, I suppose it all depends on what mood I am in! The two cards in the September and October positions will also have an influence on my decision.

I then go round the clock in sequence and do not flit from card to card as I am able to do in both the Pyramid and the Celtic Cross layout. However, the sequence has a bit of flexibility to it, and in fact this is the only spread I do where the location of the card is indeed relevant.

Just for the fun of it and to show you an example of how the Horoscope spread works I will do a reading for you, the reader of this book! It will be based on the cards in the photograph. Of course, I don't know anything about the reader of this book except that they seem to be interested in Tarot cards. To add to the difficulty, this reading will have to fit many, many of my readership! A little bit like a newspaper horoscope reading, come to think of it!

I don't guarantee the accuracy of it for obvious reasons, but at least it will show you the mechanics of how to do a Horoscope Spread. However, I also suspect it might be more accurate than you think. I discovered a long time ago that although each human being is different, we are all actually alike more than we realise. Anyway, see if it applies to you. You might just get a surprise!

Incidentally, I know that some of the cards in the photograph will be a little difficult to see—but don't worry. I know what they are even if you don't! Come to think of it, I have just realised while I am writing these words that it might be a good idea to tell you what the cards actually are! Here goes:

January: The Fool.
February: Knight of Swords.
March: Eight of Cups.
April: Ace of Swords.
May: The Sun.
June: Three of Wands.
July: Queen of Cups.
August: Seven of Wands.
September: The World.
October: Judgement.
November: Queen of Swords.
December: Five of Coins.

Now, my next problem is to figure out which month to start the reading in. I am writing this in June 2020, but alas I am not psychic enough to know when you, the reader, will be reading these words. I have therefore decided that the best thing to do is to start the reading from January 2021, which means starting at the one o'clock position. That starts with the Fool card but don't worry—it doesn't mean you are going to make a fool of yourself at the very start of the year! With the Knight of Swords adjacent in the two o'clock position (February), it indicates that in the early part of the year you will be raring to go and trying out new adventures, learning new things and ready to take advantage of new opportunities.

Interpretation

In the month of March, I see you finally coming to terms with a bad experience in the past, walking away from old traumas and putting them behind you.

The Spring and early Summer will be a really great period for you because you have some very powerful cards here, particularly the Sun card, which is the best card in the pack. I am referring to April, May and June. With the Sun card and the Sword of Victory showing up in April and May along with the Three of Wands showing you looking to new horizons in your life, this should be a good period for you. The month of July should be a very good period for matters of love, romance or marriage. You seem to be in a more settled frame of mind in these areas during this period.

You seem to be quite busy in August and working quite hard. In September you may possibly be contemplating or even taking a trip of some kind. In October and November it seems that you will be making important decisions around this time, and the good news is that if you make those decisions carefully and not impulsively, the odds are that you will make the correct decisions. In December you will be reflecting not only on the year gone by but on past events even from decades ago, sometimes sad events. There is no point revisiting the past. Yesterday is history, tomorrow is only a mystery, but today is a gift. That is why it is called the present.

There, I have just predicted the year 2021 for you. And all my readers come to think of it! I hope it works out for you!

I won't analyse this reading for you. I think it will be more educational for you perhaps to figure out what I said and why I said it. I use the cards more as a guideline for my intuition and imagination rather than strictly keeping to a specific meaning. After all, the client does not know how I am interpreting the cards and they don't need to know either. What they want are results, and the methods I am describing get results. Or at least they have for me in 33 years of reading Tarot cards at the time of writing. I expect they will for you also.

CHAPTER SEVEN
Money

Way back in Chapter Three, I decided that I would have seven chapters in this book, because seven is a number of spirituality. However, something has gone wrong somewhere, because the subject of this chapter isn't terribly spiritual. In other words, money! Even the fact that 25% of the cards in the Minor Arcana are concerned with money still doesn't quite cut it. Money just isn't terribly associated with spirituality.

To complicate matters further, because I suddenly remembered a fortune-telling party trick while writing Chapter Six, I decided to add another chapter after this one explaining how to do it. That means that I'm going to have eight chapters in this book instead of the original seven. And to complicate things even further still, eight is actually a money number in numerology, which means that this chapter should really be Chapter Eight, rather than Seven!

I suppose I had better move on before I confuse my readers any further. The subject of this chapter is the business of earning money with Tarot cards. Everyone, no matter how spiritual they are, requires money. After all, we all like to have food with our meals! It is no accident that, as I have already mentioned, there is an entire suit in the Tarot (Pentacles/Coins) which deals exclusively with financial matters and materialism generally. As the old but cynical witticism states, "Money is the root of all evil. That is why I am trying to dig it up!"

The only snag is that I am probably not the best person to pontificate about marketing Tarot services, since I am a pretty awful businessman myself. That means that this chapter may well be an example of the blind leading the blind. Still, I have managed somehow to survive since 1987 as a professional Tarot reader, so I suppose that must count for something. I do believe that at least I can tell you a few of the things I have done to bring in reasonable revenue over the years.

I suppose the first thing I should do is advise you on the best price to charge for your services. The trouble is that I don't really have an answer for that since a lot depends on what kind of readings you are doing, how long the session is, how experienced you are, what area of the country you are working and all sorts of other factors. So that is the bad news.

However, here is the good news. Although I can't tell you how much to charge, I can indeed give you an idea on the best way to figure it out. I suppose the first thing you need to do is check out the prices that other readers in your area charge to figure out the going rate. Once you do that, try this system, which was taught to me not by a Tarot card reader but by a vacuum cleaner salesman! I think it is an excellent method for figuring out what to charge for any service, not just Tarot reading.

First, you have to decide what you are worth. Be honest with yourself, not overly modest, but not overly pleased with yourself either. Just be realistic in your estimation of what you are worth. Put that fee firmly into your mind.

Your next step is to decide what is the minimum fee you will accept. This, of course, is probably a lot less than the amount you thought you were worth.

Now, the final and key step to the process is simply pricing yourself right in the middle of the two numbers you came up with. That will probably be the correct fee for your services.

My philosophy is not to overcharge because I refuse to take advantage of people's vulnerabilities. However, I also refuse to undercharge either. A happy medium (and no—I am not referring to the spiritualist kind) is the best answer.

Now, there are all sorts of ways to earn money with Tarot cards such as doing readings in New Age shops, Coffee house readings, telephone sessions, Skype readings and various types of internet readings. I have little experience in any of these options so I can't discuss them. If you are interested in any of these possibilities, then alas, you will have to read another book.

I think therefore that the best plan for me would be to describe the five areas where I *do* have experience in earning money with Tarot readings. These would be psychic fairs and kindred events, private appointments, psychic house parties, sound recorded internet readings, and last but not least, hotel readings. I will take each option in turn. First let me deal with:

Psychic Fairs And Kindred Events

I think this must be the scenario where nowadays I have made the most money. I have travelled all over Canada to work at psychic fairs and have done very well at them. At the time of writing I have cut down on them somewhat and stick to more local events simply because as I get older, I find the travel a bit wearing.

I should explain that psychic fairs in Canada are somewhat different to fairs in, say, the US and Great Britain, for example. There are similarities of course, but there are also differences. Let me take the USA first of all. I have never worked at a psychic fair in America, but from what I gather, many, or perhaps even most of them, work on a split of the revenue taken in between the reader and the promoter of the fair. There is some sort of ticket or chip system which people purchase and use to pay the psychic of their choice. At the end of the day the reader cashes in his tickets and splits the percentage with the promoter. Since I have never worked in the US, the less I say about American psychic fairs, the better. However, when I describe how I do the fairs in Canada, you may well see some aspect that would apply in the US as well.

As I indicated in the first chapter of this book, I have a tiny amount of experience in British psychic fairs. They do not use the percentage system that I just explained, but just like the Canadian fairs that I am more accustomed to, you have to pay for your booth space and the money you make is your own. I think the main difference between British psychic fairs and Canadian ones is that the hours are far less onerous. They tend to be two-day fairs rather than the three days which are normal in Canada.

Furthermore, the hours of the event are much shorter. A typical day at a British psychic fair would start at, say, 11 am, and finish at 6 pm. In Canada it would start at 11 am and finish at somewhere between 9 pm and 9.30 pm.

One other difference I seem to remember, although I don't know if it still applies nowadays, is that the waiting procedure is different. In Canada the attendees at these events write their names down on a sign-up sheet so that they can wander round the fair and come back for the reading when their reading is due, rather than having to wait around while the reader is busy with another client. In the UK I remember people would sort of sit or stand around the booth as if waiting in a doctor's waiting room. Or perhaps in some cases it was a matter of first come, first served.

Anyway, I think it is best for me to describe the Canadian procedures in these matters since that is where my experience lies. You can adapt it to your own circumstances.

Most Canadian psychic fairs last three days: Friday. Saturday and Sunday. Fridays are, generally speaking, the quietest of the three days. Saturdays and Sundays tend to be much busier, although the Sundays do have less hours to work.

At the time of writing, a booth can cost anywhere from $600 to $1000 depending on the venue and the size of the fair. There would also be travel and hotel expenses if you do not live locally, which in the majority of cases you probably won't. As you can see from this, if you don't know what you are doing, your adventure could be a financial disaster. This is one of the advantages of the US style fairs, where you pay a percentage of the revenue to the promoter. That way you don't lose money.

However, if you know how to work a psychic fair properly you can do very well indeed. Normally, if you are doing things correctly and the fair is reasonably well attended, you should have covered your booth fee plus expenses sometime during Saturday. The remainder of this day plus the Sunday should be all profit.

So, how do you do things correctly? Well, for one thing, your readings had better be good. Word of mouth is very powerful, and if one of your clients is impressed by your reading, she will no doubt tell her friends, and they in turn will be eager to have a reading from you themselves.

You should have a good banner hanging on the back of your booth and an attractive display on your front table. At this point I suppose I had better explain what a "front table" is. Just as the name suggests, this is generally a 6ft-long table at the front of the booth. You do not do your readings on this table. You have a much smaller table, such as a card table or some other small alternative at the back of the booth where you do the readings. The picture should give you an idea of what I am talking about.

In the picture you will see that I do not particularly practice what I preach when I say that on the front table you should have an attractive display. Quite frankly, many of the other readers at the fair have better displays than I do. However, I compensate for that because I have built up a considerable reputation over the years, so I don't need it that much.

Money

You will notice in the picture a lady writing something. What is happening here is that she is writing in my comment book how wonderful she thinks I am! She has already had a reading and wants to express her satisfaction by writing a positive comment.

In fact, the comment book is one of my most powerful marketing tools and does get me a massive amount of business. My own book goes back many years. I strongly recommend the use of this very effective strategy to anyone who does readings at psychic fairs and kindred events. In fact, the majority of exhibitors at these events seem to have a comment book.

It occurs to me that the photograph is going to be very useful to me in describing some of the procedures used at psychic fairs. You will notice that just to the right of the lady's hand is a sheet of paper. You will not be able to read what it says, but that's no problem because I am about to tell you anyway. The actual words are "You can record the reading on your phone if you wish".

This is another very good sales technique. Many attendees love to have their readings recorded. In fact, at one time I and other readers used to make available audiocassette tape recordings for the clients, until of course cassette tapes fell by the wayside. When that happened the readers then started to make the recordings on CDs instead, but after a while they started to become obsolete too and they didn't work in everybody's computer, so in the end I advised people to record the readings on their phones.

The trouble with that, of course, is that half the time, people don't know how to work their own phones! In the end I put a sign up as just described, saying that they could record the reading on their phone if they wished. Actually, most people don't bother, but the option is there if they wish. And some people do, of course.

To the right of the phone notice can be seen a sign-up sheet and above that is a notice saying, "Please put your name down if I am busy". That way makes it possible for people to sign up for a reading when I am occupied with a client. They just add their name to the list and people will be taken when it is their time.

Incidentally, I should have mentioned that readings at psychic fairs and kindred events usually take somewhere between twenty minutes to half an hour. If I find that I am very busy, the times of the reading are usually around twenty minutes. If business is a little quieter, I can take my time and extend the session to around thirty minutes.

Sometimes readers will use what are known as "front persons" who sit at the front table and act as a sort of secretary to the Tarot reader, answering questions when he or she is busy with a client and keeping things organised with regard to the waiting list.

I have used front persons myself with varying results. Sometimes it works out and sometimes it doesn't. The wrong front person can discourage customers whereas the right front person can encourage them. A lot depends on their personality. And, of course, one disadvantage is that you have to pay them! Having said that, many of the readers have family members fronting for them such as spouses, etc., so it all works out OK.

Psychic fairs can be exhausting and sometimes stressful because of the pressure of doing one reading after another with hardly a break. And when business slows down you have a different pressure because you now have to sell your services to the attendees. Sometimes a good front person can do this for you and sometimes you are better off doing it yourself. In truth I find the selling of the services much harder work than doing the readings themselves, although both can be pretty tough going at times. The upside of all this is that psychic fairs can be very lucrative if you know what you are doing.

I also mentioned "kindred events". By this I mean metaphysical fairs, holistic health events, home shows, craft shows, fairs, festivals, flea markets and any other venues where the general public are admitted and you pay a fee to set up a booth.

With regard to metaphysical fairs and holistic healing trade shows, they are not specifically targeted to attendees who are interested in psychic readings but to a much broader market who are interested in metaphysical matters and alternative health matters generally, although psychic readers often exhibit at these events. However, the same sort of people who attend psychic fairs tend also to attend metaphysical and holistic health shows. That means you can charge the same prices for a reading as you would at a psychic fair.

The other kind of kindred events I mentioned have to be treated a bit differently since the attendees at these venues are not there to have a reading and are not necessarily interested in Tarot or anything associated with readings of any kind. That means that you have to charge less money than you would at a psychic, metaphysical or alternative healing show. The readings should probably be a bit shorter, too. Of course, to balance this disadvantage out somewhat you won't have anywhere near the same competition from other Tarot readers and in fact you may well be the only reader at the event.

One thing you do have to be very careful of though: at psychic fairs the atmosphere is generally fairly quiet and you can do the readings without much distraction. At metaphysical and holistic events there might be some more noise around, which can make readings difficult to do.

However, worst of all from the noise element point of view are the more general events, such as home shows, fairs, festivals, etc. The worst thing that can possibly happen if you are trying to do quiet Tarot sessions is to find you are located near a stage where there is a fashion show or loud music of some kind. You are also liable to be next door to a noisy neighbour who sells some sort of noisy product and you find it difficult to work because of the racket. You must therefore be very careful when booking this type of event to explain to the organisers that you must have a location where you are away from too much noise and hopefully they will accommodate you.

Private Readings By Appointment

As I mentioned in the very first chapter, I had great success when I first started in booking readings by appointment simply by putting a classified advertisement in an Irish newspaper. However, a few years later when I tried the same tactic in a Toronto newspaper, nary a phone call!

In Ireland there were no psychic fairs when I was there (although there are nowadays), but it mattered little because I had such good results by setting up private appointments. When I moved to Toronto, it was a lot harder to build up an appointment business, one reason being is that there were so many psychics and Tarot readers in the city, whereas in Dublin there were only a tiny few competitors.

As I previously mentioned I am no businessman, so I don't really have any useful ideas as to how you would set up an appointment business. You could try advertising in the newspaper like I did and perhaps you might get more consistent results than I achieved. I imagine that if you could get a local radio or TV show of your own that would also be of considerable help. You may be one of those modern people who knows how to advertise on the internet. Not for me I am afraid since I was born in the year of the dinosaur and that stuff is quite beyond me.

I did once try out an idea suggested to me that I should go into a library and find books on the Tarot. Or in fact any metaphysical subject such as palmistry, astrology, etc., and place a business card advertising my services somewhere within the pages. The theory obviously was that only people interested in New Age topics would be looking through a book of that nature and as a result would be tempted to contact me and have a reading. They might even think the card was there as a mere bookmark.

I did try this but alas got off to a bad start because instead of trying it out in a library, I was daft enough to do it in a bookstore and placed several cards in several metaphysically inclined books. Alas, instead of getting phone calls from clients begging for readings I got a phone call from an irate bookshop owner who was not terribly pleased about the matter. After that incident I lost interest rather rapidly in the idea. However, there it is for what it is worth and if you, my reader, are foolhardy enough to try it, be my guest. You will probably get better luck in a library rather than a bookshop I imagine.

I do think the best way probably to get private appointments is old-fashioned word of mouth. The more readings you do—the more readings you do! If you give good quality readings your client will recommend you to their friends and the ball starts rolling. The way you get started is by doing the public readings at psychic fairs and kindred events as I have already mentioned. Particularly local events. Finding a flea market that you can set up at on a regular basis might work well for example. You give every single person you give a reading to your business card and flyer advertising your services and tell them that if they ever want a more in-depth private session in the future, this is where they can contact you.

I personally give the client two options if they want a private appointment: a one-hour session or a thirty-minute session. However, when I do the hour, consultation I also do palmistry and numerology, which lengthens the session. However, since this book is about the Tarot rather than these other divination systems I would recommend that you go for thirty-minute Tarot readings. Although it is indeed possible for a very experienced reader to do a full-hour Tarot session, I do believe that for most practitioners (and that includes myself) one hour of Tarot alone is just too long. One advantage of thirty-minute readings is that it becomes far more likely that your client will bring a friend along who will also require a reading. They would only have to wait thirty minutes before it was their turn, rather than an entire hour.

The question now arises as to where you do the readings. Some Tarot readers work from home. If you wish to go this route you will have to have one room which is devoted entirely to readings which is easily accessible and away from the rest of the household. It would also be desirable to decorate the room in such a way to give it a bit of a mystical atmosphere without going overboard.

You may have another business which has premises of some kind. There may be a room that could be used for readings. After all, as I described in the first chapter of this book, when I first started I used my own office premises, which were there already for my use.

You could rent your own office premises to do readings, but of course, you would have to make sure you get enough business to make it worth it. Or you could do what I do. I make an arrangement with a holistic healing centre where I can rent space for 30 minutes to an hour. If someone wants to book an appointment, I let them do it and then I contact the centre to ask for space and they find some room for me to operate in. Of course, the centre gets a cut of the action. You may well be able to find some place where you can make a similar arrangement.

These are just a few suggestions. I shall leave it to your own ingenuity to come up with something and I wish you luck with it.

Psychic House Parties

The way this works is that a number of people (usually women) have a get-together in a person's home and invite a psychic consultant to come along and give a reading to each of the guests. This can be a Tarot session or in fact any kind of divination system that the reader has expertise in.

The reading is done in a separate room in order to give the guest some privacy while the other ladies congregate in the main room, where they gossip and partake of refreshments, either alcoholic or otherwise! The sessions generally take around twenty to thirty minutes, depending on the number of guests present. Some readers will take up to twenty people!

Of course, when they take that many, the readings are usually not done in the evening but at the weekends in the daytime, so as to make more hours available for the readings. I would imagine with that many people to get through, the sessions would be shortened considerably, possibly to fifteen minutes or so for each person. Some readers even travel out of town to do these parties when they are guaranteed a large number of guests to be present.

I personally prefer to stay local and I don't particularly want to stay in a house for more than three hours, so this is my way of doing things. It may not be as lucrative as other house-party scenarios, but it suits me personally.

I insist on a minimum of three people present and a maximum of six. There of course can be more people at the event but I am referring specifically to the number of people that actually have a reading with me. Each person gets a thirty-minute reading. I find a twenty-minute reading is a bit rushed and I can give the guest more information and more help in thirty minutes that I can in twenty.

With regard to payment, the way it generally works is that each of the guests pays individually and the hostess of the party gets a free reading. However, because I take in fewer guests than other readers might and don't make as much revenue this way, I feel that I cannot afford to give the hostess a free reading, so instead I will give her a free Astrology or Tarot book instead.

The best way to promote these events is to do basically what I advised when seeking private appointments. That is, when you do public readings at flea markets, psychic fairs and other venues, you give everyone your business card and a flyer explaining that you do psychic house parties. You can also have a Tarot reading website where you proclaim the house-party service.

To close, one thing I should mention that is vitally important: make sure the first couple of readings are excellent. If they are sub par, you will be in trouble because they will go back into the main room and complain about how bad you were, and it will affect the whole evening. A domino effect will set in and they will poison the whole group. They will come in to you in a very negative manner and you will pick up their energy with far more difficulty.

It doesn't matter so much if the mediocre reading takes place near the end of the evening, because presumably people will be happy with you by then. Of course, every reading should be as good as you can make it. It is just that great harm is done if the early readings are sub par.

Sound Recorded Internet Readings

Years ago I used to offer readings by mail order. The way it worked was that the client would send me any three questions they wanted an answer to and a photograph of themselves. Plus money for the reading, of course! In return I would send them back a thirty-minute Tarot reading on a cassette audio tape.

This procedure worked out well until cassette tapes became obsolete, so as a result I gave the idea up.

However, not very long ago I discovered a sound recorder on my computer and I suspect this may well be on every computer. As indicated previously I am not overly computer savvy so I can't be 100 percent sure of this. After investigating the matter, I realised that I could do the old mail order idea. I figured that the clients could send me a photograph by email along with their three questions. They could then pay me by PayPal, credit card, or transferring the money to my bank account.

I would then record a thirty-minute reading within 24 hours of receiving payment and send it in a sound file. To illustrate my computer incompetence, I am not entirely sure if I am sending it as an MP3 file or an MP4 file, although I suspect it is probably the latter.

When I do the reading I actually use the Tarot cards and make sure the client can hear me shuffling them. Since they obviously cannot shuffle, cut and select the cards themselves as they would if it was a face-to-face, in-person reading, I have to do it on their behalf. It makes no difference to the effectiveness of the session and in fact these internet readings are very, very accurate. I think this is because I am surrounded by silence when I do the reading except for the sound of my own voice. There is nothing to distract my attention as there would be in a face to face reading and I can concentrate far better.

At first, I found difficulty in sending the file as an attachment since it was just too big. I solved that problem by using WeTransfer, which is a free service, and they send the file to the client to be downloaded. I also have a copy of the reading in my computer which I do not delete for several months just in case the client loses or deletes it accidentally.

One advantage of this type of reading is that it usually gets feedback by email from the client after it has been listened to. When seeing people face to face, naturally you often get feedback, but not in every case. The feedback does seem to be much more frequent when the reading is delivered in this electronic manner.

I have done quite a few readings in this manner and it works out very well indeed. I don't need to leave the house, so it is very convenient for both myself and the client. And it doesn't matter if they live on the other side of the world either! In short, I recommend this idea for your consideration.

Hotel Readings

I haven't done any of these for years. In fact, the last time I did them was before the age of the internet. However, I imagine they would work just as well, or perhaps even better, in this electronic age since the idea could probably be more powerfully promoted nowadays through social media.

Anyway, I will give you the bare bones of how I used to do this years ago and it was indeed quite successful. I bet some enterprising reader of this book who has an adventurous nature could have just as much success as I did.

I used to do this when I lived in Ireland. The first thing I would do is to find a small town, of which there are a great many in Ireland. The reason for a small town is that there generally would not be a lot going on there and my advertising would stand out.

After deciding on which town I would try it out in, I would find a suitable hotel to operate the idea. I would book three rooms. One room would be a conference or seminar room which would hold up to say 50 or so people, one would be a much smaller room to do private readings in and finally the last room would be for my accommodation. I would of course negotiate some deal or other (I cannot remember what) to bring the rental fees down.

Sometimes I would book this for one, sometimes two or even three days depending on how well I thought it would work. I do remember that I would operate this idea for midweek rather than the weekend.

Once the hotel booking part of things was out of the way, I would then start to promote the event. From memory I think I used to advertise it about ten days to two weeks before the big day or days.

The most important part of things was to find the local newspaper. I would usually do this on the day I booked the hotel. I would wander into their offices with a photograph and a press release, which I wrote myself, and ask for a reporter.

After doing so I informed him or her that I was a world-famous psychic or some such twaddle and would be giving a seminar on the subject in the hotel in question. I would give the newspaper scribe the photograph and the press release, which of course was a thinly disguised advertisement for my upcoming seminar.

He or she would always say that they would not promise anything, but in reality, they never, ever, even once, failed to print the story, and they usually published it word for word according to my own press release.

I should mention that when I first went into the newspaper office, I placed a couple of advertisements of which more anon; this of course improved my chances of seeing a reporter, and also of the newspaper publishing my article.

I placed a display ad and a classified ad. The display ad advertised a free seminar to be held on the appointed dates at 8pm. The important word in the ad was "FREE", which I have always considered to be a magic word. However, I also put in smaller print at the end of the ad "private interviews can be arranged".

The other advertisement was a classified ad simply stating, "Famous psychic arriving in Drogheda (or whatever town I graced with my presence). Palmist and Tarot Reader. One-hour taped session. Phone for appointment NOW," and then of course I would give my phone number. The reference to taped sessions, of course, was because, as I previously discussed, audiocassette tapes were the norm in those days. Nowadays the clients would have to record the readings on their phone.

For the phone number I would give my phone number in Dublin where I lived at the time, although the event itself would in fact be out of town. However, people didn't seem to mind calling long distance and setting up appointments. Nowadays the whole process would no doubt be a lot easier with the internet and toll-free phone numbers.

Anyway, this would mean that I would have appointments already set up before I even arrived in the town.

After I finished my business with the newspaper, my next step would be to find the local radio station if there was one. I would then pay to have some radio advertising of the event, but at the same time, arrange with the station to have a radio interview with me, which would also promote the occasion.

On the day of the event I would show up at the hotel, check in and the first thing I would do after looking at the rooms was to put up a few signs in the lobby advertising my seminar. The presentation lasted around an hour or so and was usually fairly well attended with an average of 40 people or so showing up. The chairs were arranged theatre style and I would just waffle away for an hour.

However, during the waffling period I would also announce that if anyone wanted to have a reading after I finished the lecture, I would be happy to do it there and then. Of course, they would have to pay for it. I also took the opportunity to inform everyone that if they wanted a more in-depth reading they could make an appointment to see me the next day.

I always got around 10 or so people coming up afterwards to have a brief 10 to 15-minute reading after my seminar, and of course, because it was in a large room with plenty of seats, they would sit around and wait until it was their turn.

The next day I would see people privately in the smaller room I had booked for their hour-long session.

This was quite a profitable venture and it may well be something that one of my more go-ahead readers might try their hand at. As I have already mentioned I strongly suspect it would work even better nowadays than it did way back then when I was active doing it.

CHAPTER EIGHT
A Party Trick

This is the little magic trick with a fortune-telling theme that I promised you back in Chapter Six. Consider it an amusing bonus for sticking with this book right to the end. It is not something to be taken too seriously and should be presented in a fun way.

The first thing you will have to do is to procure six blank index cards. The usual size is 4 inches by 6 inches. You now have to print up various questions on each card which I shall explain in a moment. In the old days I would type them up on the cards. I am not sure how it would be done nowadays. For all I know there might be some fancy way of doing it on a computer but I confess that I am not psychic enough to know how. You could possibly take the cards to a printer and tell them what you want. Either that or write the questions down if you can find enough space. I will let you, the reader, figure all that out for yourself. I am sure you will be cleverer than me where this is concerned.

One of those cards will be the main card. I shall call it the master card (nothing to do with the well-known credit card!), and you will print out thirty questions on that card. The questions should be printed in single space so as to fit onto the card. The other five cards have only fifteen questions on them, thus taking up less space, so these should be printed in double space. Each of the cards should be numbered at the top. Thus the master card should not be numbered, but the rest of the cards should be numbered one, two, three, four, and five, respectively. These numbers at the top are very important to the working of the trick as will be seen once I get into the explanation.

Let me deal with the master card first. Here are the thirty questions:

1. Will there ever be peace in the world?
2. Will I win the lawsuit?
3. When will I get married?
4. Will I get out of this mess?
5. Will I get the money?

6. Should I tell all?
7. Am I easily deceived?
8. Should I borrow the money?
9. Will I be taking a journey?
10. Is my partner in life true to me?
11. Will my health improve?
12. Will I be successful?
13. What is my greatest fault?
14. Should I believe all I hear?
15. When will I get a job?
'17. When will I retire?
18. Should I go on a diet?
19. Should I sell the property?
20. Should I change my job?
21. Will I take an ocean voyage?
22. How many children will I have?
23. Should I sign the papers?
24. Should I take out insurance?
25. Will the operation be a success?
26. Can I afford a vacation?
27. Will I be wealthy?
28. Will I buy a new car?
29. Should I offer to help?
30. Have I any enemies?

Now we go on to card number one. Not quite so many questions this time:

1. Will there ever be peace in the world?
2. When will I get married?
3. Will I get the money?
4. Am I easily deceived?
5. Will I be taking a journey?
6. Will my health improve?
7. What is my greatest fault?
8. When will I get a job?
9. When will I retire?
10. Should I sell the property?

11. Will I take an ocean voyage?
12. Should I sign the papers?
13. Will the operation be a success?
14. Will I be wealthy?
15. Should I offer to help?

Now for card number two:

1. Will I win the lawsuit?
2. When will I get married?
3. Should I tell all?
4. Am I easily deceived?
5. Is my partner in life true to me?
6. Will my health improve
7. Should I believe all I hear?
8. When will I get a job?
9. Should I go on a diet?
10. Should I sell the property?
11. How many children will I have?
12. Should I sign the papers?
13. Can I afford a vacation?
14. Will I be wealthy?
15. Have I any enemies?

Card number three:

1. Will I get out of this mess?
2. Will I get the money?
3. Should I tell all?
4. Am I easily deceived?
5. Will I be successful?
6. What is my greatest fault?
7. Should I believe all I hear?
8. When will I get a job?
9. Should I change my job?
10. Will I take an ocean voyage?
11. How many children will I have?
12. Should I sign the papers?
13. Will I buy a new car?

14. Should I offer to help?
15. Have I any enemies?

Card number four:

1. Should I borrow the money?
2. Will I be taking a journey?
3. Is my partner in life true to me?
4. Will my health improve?
5. Will I be successful?
6. What is my greatest fault?
7. Should I believe all I hear?
8. When will I get a job?
9. Should I take out insurance?
10. Will the operation be a success?
11. Can I afford a vacation?
12. Will I be wealthy?
13. Will I buy a new car?
14. Should I offer to help?
15. Have I any enemies?

Card number five:

1. Will I keep the date?
2. When will I retire?
3. Should I go on a diet?
4. Should I sell the property?
5. Should I change my job?
6. Will I take an ocean voyage?
7. How many children will I have?
8. Should I sign the papers?
9. Should I take out insurance?
10. Will the operation be a success?
11. Can I afford a vacation?
12. Will I be wealthy?
13. Will I buy a new car?
14. Should I offer to help?
15. Have I any enemies?

A Party Trick

And now for the performance! Let us assume your volunteer is a lady. Give her the master list and ask her to mentally select any of the questions thereon and concentrate on it for the moment. She does not reveal the question to you out loud but just keeps it to herself. Once this has happened take the master list from her and give her any one of the other five cards. She should look the card over and if she sees the same question again, she holds on to the card. If, however, the question is not on the card then she hands it back to you.

You repeat this procedure with the remaining four cards. If she sees the question she keeps the card and if she doesn't see it she hands the card back to you.

You are now in a position to secretly divine her question because you will know what it is! No mindreading or psychic ability necessary!

And now for the secret!

The first thing you must do is affix a numerical value to each of the five cards which are not the master card. The values for cards number one and two are easy to remember because the value for card number 1 is one and the value for card number two is two! That was easy, wasn't it? Alas, the values for cards number three, four and five are a bit more complicated. Card number three has a value of 4, card number four has a value of 8, and card number five has a value of 16.

This little chart should make it easier to follow and remember:

Card number one = 1
Card number two = 2
Card number three = 4
Card number four = 8
Card number five = 16

With a little practice you should be able to remember which number applies to which card. In actual fact, the value of each card is twice that of the preceding card.

When your volunteer hands you the cards that do not contain her question, you can easily work out which cards she still holds. For example, if she thinks of "Should I sell the property?" on the master list that means she will keep cards one, two and five and hand you cards three and four. It will not be hard for you to work out which cards she still holds.

Now, you will remember that cards one, two and five have a value of 1, 2 and 16, respectively. If you add up all three numbers you will find that the total is nineteen. All you have to do now is look at the master list and look up question nineteen. Lo and behold it will be the one concerning the property matter!

Here is another example. Let us assume she selects question 22 on the master list, which is "How many children will I have?" You take the master list from her and hand her each of the other five cards in turn. She will keep cards two, three and five and hand you cards one and four. You will quickly realise which cards she has kept and you know the values of cards two, three and five are 2, 4, and 16. If two, four and sixteen are added together, the total is 22. If you look up question 22 on the master card you will see the question refers to children.

You are now in a position to amaze the volunteer and the assembled multitude by answering the question the lady has in mind. I think it is best not to announce the question itself but to answer it in such a way as to make it obvious that you know what it is. I would advise answering it in a humorous manner since there is always a danger that someone could take your response too seriously. I would even go so far as ultimately to let people know that you are merely doing a party trick and that you are not really psychic. Let them realise that it is just a bit of fun and that you can't really read minds.

Of course, you could always do a Tarot card reading as taught in this book to answer the question! Still, I don't think that is wise. Just do it as a party trick and have some fun with it.

There's plenty of time for the serious stuff, which should be reasonably plentiful in the preceding pages. With that I now bid you good health, good luck and goodbye!

www.ingramcontent.com/pod-product-compliance
Lightning Source LLC
Chambersburg PA
CBHW061248230426
43663CB00021B/2941